DAY TRIPS
FROM CALGARY

Best of Alberta

DAY TRIPS
FROM CALGARY

REVISED EDITION

Bill Corbett

whitecap

For Teresa

Edited by Elaine Jones
Proofread by Marial Shea
Cover design by Roberta Batchelor
Cover photograph by Dave Nunuk/firstlight.ca
Interior design by Warren Clark
Interior photographs by Bill Corbett unless noted
Maps by Leslie Bell

Printed and bound in Canada

National Library of Canada Cataloguing in Publication Data

Corbett, Bill
    Best of Alberta

    Includes index.
    ISBN 1-55285-349-7

    1. Calgary Region (Alta.)—Guidebooks. I. Title.
FC3697.18.C67 2002   917.123'38043   C2002-910194-8
F1079.5.C35C67 2002

The publisher acknowledges the support of the Canada Council for the Arts and the Cultural Services Branch of the Government of British Columbia for our publishing program. We acknowledge the financial support of the Government of Canada through the Book Publishing Industry Development Program for our publishing activities.

Contents

2. North of Calgary 83

3. East of Calgary 135

Preface

The advice passed down for generations has been this: go west. Thus armed, countless residents of, and visitors to, Calgary have made a beeline for the mecca that is Banff. Banff is, and hopefully always will be, a splendid destination for Calgarians and first-time visitors to the Rocky Mountains. So, too, is the mountain splendour of nearby Kananaskis Country. But there are other places that beckon, albeit more subtly than the seductive peaks on the skyline.

I wrote this book to entice Calgary residents and visitors to consider all directions of the compass when embarking on a day trip from the city. Those who do will be wonderfully surprised.

Calgarians have at their doorstep some of the most spectacular and varied landscapes in the world. These include the fantastically shaped badlands of Drumheller, the sublime ranchlands of Millarville, the rolling hills of Rumsey, the cottonwood forests of Lethbridge, the prairies and pelicans of Brooks, and the foothills of Pincher Creek, to name a few. Where else could one hop in the car and in the space of an hour travel from prairies to foothills to mountains, or find all three ecosystems merged in one location?

The southern half of Alberta is also rich in human history. It dates from prehistoric hunters of 10,000 years ago and extends through the millennia when natives and buffalo ruled the landscape. More recently, it covers the eras of white explorers and fur traders, whisky traders and Mounties, ranchers and settlers. These and other stories are well told in myriad small-town museums and the multi-million-dollar interpretive facilities that attract visitors from around the world.

The premise of this book is simple—what can you see and do within a two-hour drive in any direction from Calgary? Some destinations can be reached in 20 minutes, others in a full two hours.

Many of the farthest destinations have much to offer along the way. In such cases, I have described the trip as much as the destination. If you think Lethbridge or the Crowsnest Pass is too distant for a day trip, consider the number of tourists willing to make a day's pilgrimage to Lake Louise, which is almost two hours from the city.

This is not a wilderness guide, though you might well find solitude on many of these trips, especially if you chart your own course on back roads. The prairies have been ploughed, the foothills claimed by ranches and acreages, and the mountains marked by tourist developments. But there are still tracts of native prairie, patches of aspen parkland, and numerous other unspoiled areas protected within parks or natural reserves. Even the altered landscape still possesses the power to inspire with its varied topography and distant vistas.

This latest edition of *Day Trips from Calgary* includes nine new trips plus a colour photo section. The new trips range from watching a golden eagle migration and RCMP dogs in training to exploring the rugged Ghost River Valley and the historically arresting town of Lacombe. There are also some longer hikes—to gain lofty views from the shoulder of Yamnuska, see alpine larches in autumn and visit the splendid fossil beds of the Burgess Shale.

The trips described in this book can be enjoyed by families, seniors, avid naturalists, and anyone interested in places and people. Many are loop trips or offer alternative return routes to the city. While the automobile is the primary means of touring this country, there are lots of opportunities to stretch your legs. Wherever possible, I have included a short, often interpretive, walk of usually no more than a kilometre or two in length.

These trips require no expertise and no special equipment other than a tank of gas, a road map, perhaps a picnic lunch, and a plentiful supply of curiosity. Enjoy.

Acknowledgements

Researching and writing a wide-ranging book such as this would not have been possible without the assistance of many people. While I travelled all the routes described in this book, it was sometimes in the company of others, who patiently put up with all the stops and detours along the way. Others suggested excellent trips that would otherwise have been bypassed. I am especially indebted to the expertise of geologists, geographers, historians, and naturalists who answered my queries and proofread parts of the text.

These contributors include Kelly Adams, Leslie Bell, Helen Corbett, Don Cockerton, Graeme Dales, Anne Elton, Jacquie Gilson, Chris Harvie, Peter Jones, Ed Jurewicz, David May, Forbes and Di Macdonald, Sharon Macfarlane, Paul McNeil, Teresa Michalak, Peter Reed, Jim Robertson, Fenn Roessingh, Bob Sharpe, Peter Sherrington, Nancy and Dennis Stefani, Stacey Steil, Lawrence Tanner, Cliff Wallis, Cleve Wershler and Brendan Wilson, and my editors, Linda Ostrowalker and Elaine Jones. I would also like to thank the staff of Kananaskis Country, the Canadian Parks Service, and the numerous people working in the small museums and information centres of southern and central Alberta who provided information and documents.

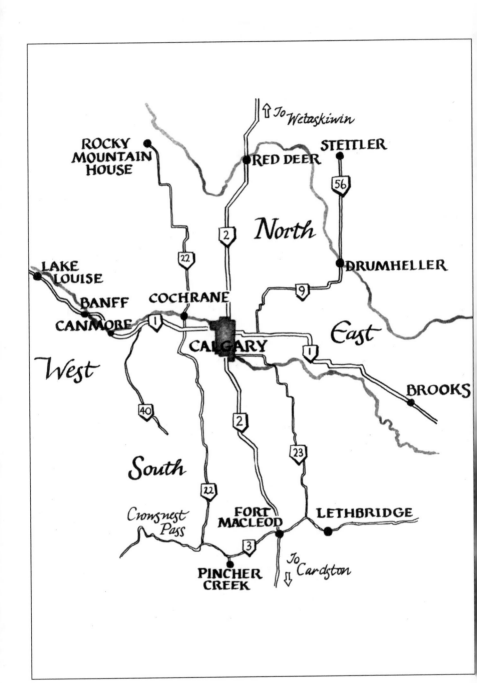

Introduction
How to Use This Guide

The trips covered in this book are divided into four sections that roughly correspond with the directions of the compass, using Calgary as a centre. In some cases the dividing line has been somewhat arbitrarily drawn for organizational purposes. Thus, you will find Cochrane listed in the West, because it follows the Bow Valley, while the nearby Big Hill Springs Provincial Park is in the North.

Each section begins with a brief overview of the geographical area and what it offers the day tripper. The trips that follow are generally listed in order of their proximity to Calgary. In cases where there are several trips of equal distance from Calgary, I have arranged them in geographical groups so that those who desire longer expeditions can easily combine several trips at once.

With a couple of exceptions, all the destinations in this book can be reached within two hours of driving at highway speeds. Anything longer, to my mind, constitutes an overnight trip. In fact, some may even feel the longer trips included here are already pushing the limits of an easy day trip. For that reason, I have excluded such worthy areas as Medicine Hat, Cypress Hills, Writing-On-Stone Provincial Park, and Waterton Lakes National Park.

Some destinations have sufficient attractions to warrant

several day trips. These include Lethbridge, Brooks, Drumheller, Banff, and Red Deer. For such destinations, I have usually given a brief introduction to the area, city, or town and then described several trips, some of which can be combined by ambitious day trippers or overnight visitors. I have also described, as trips, the major highway approaches to these destinations.

The following bold-faced designations are at the top of each trip report.

ROUTE: This describes, often in some detail, the chosen route to a destination or the roads followed on loop trips. Obviously, alternatives are available in many cases, and I encourage people to take detours whenever the urge strikes. Where several trips are grouped in one area, I have tried to provide a different approach or return for each, so as to expose day trippers to as much country-side as possible. All route descriptions begin from the part of Calgary nearest to the destination or route. People will choose various approaches through the city to get to the city limits. And if someone lives, say, on the western outskirts of Calgary, they are unlikely to head to the city centre to begin a trip to Banff.

DRIVING DISTANCE: These are approximate distances, either one way to a desti-nation or round trip on loop routes. They do not include side trips or driving around the area of the destination. The distances are provided to give day trip-pers a rough idea of how much time will be involved in driving, a particular concern of parents with young children. In all cases, the distances are meas-ured from the edge of the city, so allow for driving time to and from your point of departure within Calgary.

NOTES: These provide details on the operating hours and seasons of museums, information centres, and other attractions described in the trips. Remember, this was the information listed at the time of writing. Hours of operation change and attractions that were once free sometimes start charging admis-sion. It's best to phone the listed number in advance of trips that rely on visit-ing these sites. Hiking distances are listed in this section.

All the trips can be comfortably managed by the average fam-ily. Interpretive walks are usually no longer than 1.5 kilometres and are on relatively level terrain. Longer and steeper hikes are described as such.

The trip descriptions are fairly straightforward. In the first paragraph or two, I try to summarize what makes the trip worthwhile and list the highlights. The body of the trip report covers what one can expect to see and do, not only at the destination but also along the way.

Useful Phone Numbers

Note: These are local calls from Calgary unless otherwise indicated with the prefix (403).

Alberta Economic Development & Tourism - toll-free
travel information and trip planning 1-800-661-8888.
Calgary Convention and Visitors Bureau 263-8510.
Kananaskis Country - Canmore head office
(403) 678-5508.
Parks Canada - Calgary regional headquarters 292-4401.
Banff Visitor Centre (403) 762-1550.
Lake Louise Visitor Centre (403) 522-3833.
Chinook Country Tourist Association - Lethbridge
1-800-661-1222.
Big Country Tourist Association - Drumheller
(403) 823-5885.
David Thompson Country Tourist Council - Red Deer
1-888-244-1400.
Battle River Tourist Association - Camrose
(403) 672-8555.
Environment Canada - Calgary-Banff recorded weather
299-7878.
Alberta Motor Association - 24-hour road reports
246-5853.
Government of Alberta Rite Line - toll-free access to
provincially run facilties such as Royal Tyrrell Museum
of Palaeontology or Frank Slide Interpretive Centre
310-0000.

South

South of Calgary

For my money, the area stretching south of Calgary has the most diversity to offer the day tripper. Here one can discover prairies, foothills and the front ranges of the Rocky Mountains—sometimes all in one outing. The terrain is undulating and open, providing the sweeping views for which southern Alberta is famous. Southern Alberta is also noted for its chinook winds, which produce dramatic skies and brush the landscape clear of snow much of the winter.

The rolling countryside southwest of Calgary has much to offer those with only a few hours to spare. In less than half a day, you can easily scramble on the Big Rock near Okotoks, tour the aspen parkland of the Cross Conservation Area, visit the historic Turner Valley petroleum fields, marvel at the views from the lofty Leighton Centre or shop at the Millarville Farmers' Market.

The area west of Highway 2 also contains much of southern Alberta's rich ranching tradition. Most of the early big ranches were located in these rolling plains and foothills, where cattle could graze on lands once roamed by huge herds of buffalo. The big ranches were established in the early 1880s, principally by British or eastern Canadian aristocrats, who could obtain leases of up to 100,000 acres (40,470 hectares) for an annual fee of one cent per acre. While those big spreads were long ago carved up, the ranching heritage is still alive and evident on many of the southwestern trips.

The landscape east of Highway 2 lacks foothills and mountains, but the high plains of the south have much to offer to the discerning eye, especially where they are cut by coulees and deep river valleys. This area is also rich in history. The southern plains, once dominated by the Blackfoot Nation, saw the arrival in the late 1860s of the notorious American whisky traders and, soon thereafter, the North-West Mounted Police, who cleared the way for settlement. The Lethbridge area was the scene of the first irrigation farming and some of the earliest coal mining in Alberta.

All this history is well told at museums that include the world-class Head-Smashed-In Buffalo Jump, the Remington-Alberta Carriage Museum in Cardston and the Frank Slide Interpretive Centre in the Crowsnest Pass. For those looking for the finest in history and scenery, it would be hard to beat the Crowsnest Pass area.

Ann and Sandy Cross Conservation Area

ROUTE: From its intersection with Anderson Road S.W., drive south on 37 Street/Secondary 773 for 6.5 kilometres and west on Highway 22X for 6.5 kilometres to 160 Street. A 1.6-kilometre gravel road leads south to a parking area. Highway 22X can also be reached via an interchange on Deerfoot Trail/Highway 2.

DRIVING DISTANCE: 15 kilometres one way.

NOTE: The Cross Conservation Area is open to the public but only by phoning 931-9001 at least one day in advance and leaving a message as to the date of visit and size of party. Detailed instructions are provided on the answering machine message.

Imagine a landscape with substantial tracts of native prairie and dense woodlands populated by elk, deer and moose. Believe it or not, such a natural preserve exists just five minutes from Calgary's city limits. Better yet, this property and its

Students studying native prairie grasses at Ann and Sandy Cross Conservation Area.

20 kilometres of trails and sweeping views are open to the public.

The Ann and Sandy Cross Conservation Area is a 1,943-hectare parcel of rolling foothills parkland southwest of Calgary. In 1987, the Crosses donated the land to the province; it was one of the largest such gifts in Canadian history. The Nature Conservancy of Canada is the property manager, charged with preserving the area's natural habitats in perpetuity and providing conservation education, primarily to school groups.

The conservation area is situated in a transition zone between the prairies and foothills. Thus, native grasses and wildflowers on dry, sunny slopes are interspersed with aspen woodlands on shaded aspects. Spruce and willows grow in the moist valley bottoms. This biological diversity provides habitat for a variety of wildlife including elk, deer, moose, coyote, beaver, the odd bear and cougar, and, in the skies, mountain bluebirds, red-tailed hawks and great horned owls.

Less than 10 per cent of Alberta's native fescue grassland is still intact. But here there are considerable slopes of knee-high rough fescue and parry's oat grasses, where bison once grazed. These grasslands and woodlands are still largely intact, thanks to topography and good management.

Once part of Stoney Indian territory, the Cross Conservation lands were first settled in the 1880s. A succession of farmers ploughed and planted the flat hilltops and wide valley bottoms, where the invasion of non-native brome grasses, used for hay and pasture, is still evident. But the hillsides of this rolling terrain were largely left unploughed.

Sandy Cross bought the property in the 1940s and 1950s. As interested in conservation as ranching, he grazed his cattle lightly on the native grasses and delighted in the browsing herds of elk and deer. The Crosses, who continue to live on adjacent lands, are part of a well-known Calgary family with extensive ranch holdings south of the city. Sandy's father, A.E. Cross, started the A7 ranch in 1885 and later launched the Calgary Brewing and Malting Company. He was one of the four founders of the Calgary Stampede.

The 4.8-kilometre Fescue Trail is perhaps the most diverse of the several loop walks in the Cross Conservation Area. A rough track, it descends a prairie hillside ablaze in late spring and early summer with such wildflowers as sticky geranium, mouse-eared chickweed and old-man's whiskers. The trail then enters a mature forest of aspen poplar with an understorey of cow parsnip in wet places.

Here, you might encounter a herd of elk, which the Shawnee people called *wapiti* for their white rumps. Those accustomed to the often docile beasts along the highway near Banff may well be startled by a string of uncivilized cow elk crashing through the trees. In winter, the elk herd can exceed 150 animals. Safe from bow hunters on these protected lands, they can graze on the often windswept grasses and retreat to the woods for shelter and to browse on shrubs and the buds (and occasionally the bark) of aspen trees.

The mix of forest and prairie also favours aerial predators such as the red-tailed hawk and great horned owl. Indeed, this general area southwest of Calgary is believed to have the highest concentration of red-tailed hawks in North America. These birds usually nest and perch on the edge of woodlands, where they can easily prey on the Richardson's ground squirrels, mice and voles of the grasslands. The abundance of ground squirrels is obvious to anyone trying to avoid these suicidal animals on country roads in late spring and early summer.

The trail rises out of the forest to a viewpoint overlooking a sprawl of rolling ranchland and, below, the dammed ponds of Pine Creek. To the west, the front range mountains of the Rockies peek over a forested ridge. The route then loops back along the crest of the hill past relics of ranching and farming. On the return route along a grassy plateau to the parking lot, the view encompasses acreages to the north, the flattened prairie to the east and the sprawling suburbs and downtown skyline of Calgary to the northeast.

Other recommended trails are the 3.5-kilometre Aspen loop and a flat gravel trail (1 kilometre, one way) to a mountain view lookout. Remember, these lands have been preserved in a largely natural state by the careful stewardship of previous owners like the Crosses. Treat them with similar respect by staying on the trails and not picking the wildflowers or native grasses.

Leighton Centre

ROUTE: From its intersection with Anderson Road S.W., follow 37 Street/Secondary 773 south across Highway 22X. Turn west on 266 Avenue, a winding gravel road that leads to Leighton Centre.
DRIVING DISTANCE: About 22 kilometres one way.
NOTE: Leighton Centre is generally open to public viewing 10:00 a.m. to 4:00 p.m., Monday to Friday. Phone 931-3633.

The stunning view of foothills and mountains from the lawn of Leighton Centre is enough to inspire anyone to reach for a sketchbook and pencil. It's fitting that this centre is dedicated to the fine arts and particularly the expression of landscape.

This lovely trip just southwest of Calgary requires a few hours at most and leaves visitors refreshed by its splendour. At Leighton Centre, you can tour the grounds, look in on a children's art class and view the art collection adorning the rooms of the charming former residence of A.C. and Barbara Leighton. You might even decide to purchase a painting left by one of the visiting artists.

Leighton Centre is located on 32 hectares of rolling foothills overlooking the Millarville valley. The view from this lofty perch, at the same elevation as Banff townsite, takes in a panorama of nearly 500 kilometres on a clear day. Because of its height and hills, much of the land was never ploughed and thus retains an impressive cover of native grasses and wildflowers.

Founded by artist Barbara Leighton, the centre is a non-profit organization created in 1974 to celebrate and stimulate landscape art in a natural setting. The centre, run by the Leighton Foundation, offers school and summer camp programs in the restored 1919 Ballyhamage schoolhouse, moved here from a nearby site. Each year, thousands of area children receive instruction in a variety of arts and crafts that usually have a nature theme.

Professionals from around the world attend visiting artist programs, in which they produce art inspired by the area. In June and September, local professional and amateur artists are invited to one-day workshops to paint the landscape from the Leighton property. A number of adult education courses in the arts are also held in the spring and fall.

The residence, with its church-like tower, contains an extensive collection of noted artist A.C. Leighton's paintings. Various rooms also showcase the work of other landscape artists, many of them Albertans, and the sale pieces of visiting artists. Barbara Leighton believed people could relate better to paintings in a home than a gallery or museum.

A.C. Leighton was born in England and came to Canada in the 1920s, painting mountain landscapes to promote tourism for the Canadian Pacific Railway. He was later head of the Alberta College of Art in Calgary and was involved in starting the Banff School of Fine Arts. After extensive travelling, A.C. and Barbara returned to live on this land southwest of Calgary until his death in 1965. A reclusive Canadian artist who frequently sketched and painted from his yard, he is best remembered for his mountain watercolours.

Following A.C.'s death, Barbara incorporated his unsold paintings into the Leighton Foundation. She returned to school to earn a diploma in fine arts and later established a school for arts and crafts, a forerunner to today's centre. After her death in 1986, the property, house and a private art collection were added to the foundation, which is financially assisted by provincial and regional art boards.

Millarville Loop

ROUTE: From its intersection with Anderson Road S.W., drive 6.5 kilometres south on 37 Street/Secondary 773. Head west on Highway 22X for 11.5 kilometres and 13 kilometres south on Highway 22. Secondary 549 east provides access in 2.2 kilometres to the Millarville Race Track and Farmers' Market.
DRIVING DISTANCE: About 33 kilometres to Millarville and 90 kilometres round trip.
NOTE: The Millarville Farmers' Market is open 8:30 a.m. to noon, Saturdays, from mid-June to early October. Phone 931-2404.

This is a superb summer outing to the historic ranching community of Millarville. In a short day, you can shop at the famous Millarville Farmers' Market, visit several historic buildings and walk through the woods of a new provincial park. The market is only open Saturday mornings, and you should try to get there early. In this early-rising ranching country, the market is usually crowded by 10:00 a.m.

The Millarville area was first settled by the two Fisher brothers, who lived in a creekside dugout before claiming a homestead in 1884. Despite this primitive beginning, the community that evolved was by no means an expression of the Wild West. Many of the early residents were members of the British upper and middle classes, attracted to the benchlands of Threepoint Creek and the mountain views. These genteel folk loved horses perhaps more than ranching and delighted in the civilized pursuits of polo, horse races, lawn tennis and dances at Rancher's Hall.

To the south, along the Sheep River, was the Quorn ranch, established in 1886 by a syndicate of wealthy British sportsmen interested in raising purebred cattle and horses, the latter used for hunting in England. Operated in an extravagant

Millarville's Christ Church, with its unusual vertical log construction.

and leisurely manner, the ranch soon failed, and the remainder of its prize stock was sold at a loss to local markets.

While the British gentry have disappeared, their leisure activities have been preserved. Every year except for two since 1905, the locals have gathered at the Millarville Race Track for the July 1 horse races. The big event is the stock horse challenge, in which area residents race their saddle horses in hopes of winning a silver cup and belt buckle. Polo grounds can also be found on some area ranches.

The big attraction, though, is the weekly Millarville Farmers' Market, arguably the most famous in Alberta. This has everything a farmers' market should need: history, diversity and rural charm. Set among tall poplars on the racetrack grounds, the market offers a wide selection of farm-grown produce and homemade crafts, foods and other products. At least half the fun is the entertainment. On any given Saturday, there might be wagon rides, llamas on display, a rancher's breakfast, a choir singing on the lawn or a blacksmith pounding out horseshoes.

About 5 kilometres east of the race track on Secondary 549 is Millarville's historic Christ Church, one of the most striking examples of pioneer architecture in Alberta's foothills. Completed in 1896, the church is unique in its use of vertically set spruce logs. Defying the predictions of early sceptics, the church is still standing and providing Anglican services every Sunday to congregations of up to a hundred people. Many of the area's early settlers are buried in the adjacent cemetery.

Continue the tour by returning to Highway 22, driving 3.2 kilometres south, and turning west on Secondary 549. This road soon passes Millarville, a small collection of buildings that includes a 1926 general store.

Just beyond Millarville is MacKay Place, where a restored 1895 ranch house is now a charming restaurant and pub. The property also contains a tiny homestead shack built in 1886 by John Turner, for whom the nearby town of Turner Valley is named. The restaurant contains a framed homesteader's lament, no doubt shared by Turner:

> *I've been lonesome ever since I came to Millarville,*
> *All because you aren't along.*

A recent addition to the MacKay Place is a transported cabin, built in 1888 and believed to have been once used as a North-West Mounted Police detachment.

Continue west on 549, which climbs past oil pumpjacks and through more heavily wooded hills of aspen and spruce before descending into rolling ranchland. At an intersection, head north on Secondary 762 for 5.7 kilometres and then

turn right on Plummers Road. Continue for 2.9 kilometres to Brown-Lowery Provincial Park, an unexpected refuge of greenery in this ranching country.

The 228-hectare park is a lovely preserve of old-growth spruce and aspen forest with an extensive understorey of wildflowers and other plants. In low-lying areas, marshes fed by tiny streams support wetland vegetation including cow parsnips. A series of rough trails wind through the property, donated to the province by Home Oil in the 1960s. The site, previously a recreation area, became a provincial park in 1993. Its name honours two pioneers of Alberta's oil industry, Robert Brown, Sr. and James Lowery, who took part in the early development of the nearby Turner Valley oil field.

From the park, Plummers Road continues its winding course east. At a junction, turn left if you wish to pass through Priddis, located on the banks of Fish Creek. The hamlet, named after settler Charles Priddis, contains a general store, community hall and a post office housed in an old schoolhouse. Each July, Priddis hosts a Calgary Stampede breakfast that attracts crowds of some 1,500 people.

The area between Priddis and Bragg Creek, to the west, once contained a glacial lake, formed by melting mountain glaciers ponded in valleys behind the continental ice sheet to the east. Much of this valley is underlain by lake deposits from more than 10,000 years ago. The rolling hills to the southeast are part of the Priddis Uplands, which emerged from under a cover of ice as the glaciers began to stagnate. The disintegrating ice created the hummocky knob and kettle topography one sees today north of Millarville.

Okotoks-Turner Valley Loop

ROUTE: From the Highway 22X overpass, drive 12 kilometres south on Highway 2 and take Highway 2A for 8 kilometres to Okotoks. From the traffic light in downtown Okotoks, drive 2.8 kilometres south on Highway 2A and 7 kilometres west on Highway 7 to the Big Rock. Continue west through Black Diamond to Turner Valley. Return to Calgary via Highway 22 north and 22X east.

DRIVING DISTANCE: About 90 kilometres return.

NOTE: Daily tours of the historic Turner Valley Gas Plant are offered from 10:00 a.m. to 6:00 p.m., May to September. Meet at the Turner Valley Tourist Information Centre. Phone 933-4944.

This is a wonderful tour of the rolling countryside southwest of Calgary. In a few hours, one can tour the burgeoning town of Okotoks, clamber on an enormous glacial erratic called Big Rock and discover how oil was struck at Turner Valley.

Situated in the Sheep River Valley, Okotoks is the largest urban centre between Calgary and Lethbridge. Its population of some 10,000 people is fed by commuters who enjoy spectacular foothills and mountain scenery along with the relative quiet of a town 15 minutes from the big city.

In the 1880s, Okotoks was an important stopping point for travellers on the old Macleod Trail, the horse and wagon route that connected the North-West Mounted Police posts of Fort Calgary and Fort Macleod. Here, where wagons crossed the Sheep River, horses were changed and travellers spent the night at a stopping house.

The Macleod Trail, following old aboriginal routes, fell into disuse in the early 1890s, when the Canadian Pacific Railway built a spur line south from Calgary. The railway brought settlers, businesses and prosperity to Okotoks. For many years, the main employer in town was the Lineham Lumber Company, which harvested timber from leases on the upper Sheep and Highwood rivers.

Many businesses faltered after the pre-World War I boom, but the railway remained an important link to Calgary, with four passenger trains a day heading for the big city in the 1930s. The passenger service was discontinued in 1971, the victim of a high-speed highway to the east of Okotoks.

The Big Rock, near Okotoks, is the largest glacial erratic in North America.

While in the downtown area, it's worth touring the historic buildings and houses, many built from local sandstone and brick at the turn of the century. Ask for a tour map at the visitor centre, located in the old train station. Perhaps the most interesting building is the former post office, now a French restaurant, its exterior clad with pressed tin.

Many Calgarians make weekend treks to Okotoks to shop and dine at such places as the historic Creamery and the Victorian-style Ginger Tea Room and Gift Shop. Diners can work off the calories by walking the trails along the flood plain of the Sheep River, long called Sheep Creek by locals. This moist valley bottom supports tall stands of cottonwood trees and an understorey of fragrant wolf willow and saskatoon bushes.

The road southwest of Okotoks passes through magnificent rolling farm and ranchland sufficiently devoid of trees to offer extensive mountain views. Here's where I'd invest in an acreage.

On the left, it's a surprise to suddenly see two huge boulders in the middle of a farmer's field. This is the famed Big Rock, the first natural feature in Alberta to be declared a historic site. The other surprise is that the rocks are made of quartzite, which is quite unlike the underlying bedrock of sandstone and shale. The Big Rock is, in fact, an import.

Its story begins 35,000 years ago, when a landslide near the town of Jasper deposited millions of tons of rocks onto the surface of a glacier advancing east down the Athabasca Valley. Emerging from the mountains, the glacier was deflected southeast along the foothills by the massive Laurentide ice mass, advancing west from the centre of the continent. As the ice melted, tens of thousands of pinkish and purplish quartzite rocks were deposited in a narrow zone from Jasper National Park to south of the U.S. border. Collectively, these rocks are known as the Foothills Erratic Train.

At 18,000 tons, the Big Rock is the largest glacial erratic in North America. Aboriginal people, who likely used this landmark as a meeting place, called it *okatoksituktai*, meaning "where the big rock lays." The erratic was noted in 1863 by James Hector, the geologist with the Palliser Expedition, which explored much of the Canadian west.

Today, families, photographers, and even formally attired wedding parties take the short walk from a parking area to admire this fractured beauty. The 9-metre-high Big Rock is also a favourite destination for Calgary-area climbers wishing to polish their bouldering skills on the solid quartzite rock.

Continuing west, the route crosses the Sheep River again at the western outskirts of Black Diamond, named for its coal-mining past. The excavation scars of an old coal mine are visible along the banks near the bridge. The mine was opened at the turn of the century after a surveyor discovered a coal seam while digging an irrigation ditch. The coal was primarily used to heat houses.

Close by to the west is the historic town of Turner Valley.

Seepages of gas found along Sheep Creek prompted the 1914 drilling of a well that produced gas pure enough to fuel cars at the site. The ensuing boom saw the formation of 500 oil companies and wild stock speculation, but it was short-lived. Subsequent discoveries of wet gas in 1924 and oil in 1936 sparked other booms that paved the way for the development of Calgary's oil industry.

On the south side of town, gas seeping around the casing of an early well has been lit for safety reasons to produce a constant flame. During earlier boom times, the light from flared and unwanted gas could be seen 50 kilometres away in Calgary. The nearby Turner Valley Gas Plant National Historic Site, now being restored, offers free summer tours of its complex of tanks, pipelines, domed buildings and scrubbing chimneys dating back to 1933.

Sheep River Valley

ROUTE: From its junction with Macleod Trail/Highway 2, drive 17 kilometres west on Highway 22X and then 27 kilometres south on Highway 22 to Turner Valley. Turn right on Secondary 546, which is followed to its terminus at Junction Creek Campground.
DRIVING DISTANCE: About 85 kilometres one way.
NOTE: Secondary 546 west of the Sandy McNabb Campground is closed December 1 to May 14 to protect the wintering herd of bighorn sheep.

The Sheep River Valley is named for the sizable herds of bighorn sheep that have long frequented its upper slopes. Early aboriginal people called the area *itou-kai-you,* meaning "sheep at the head of the river." Archaeological evidence indicates these early inhabitants first ventured into the valley more than 7,000 years ago in search of game and shelter.

Today, much of this superb upper valley is situated in Kananaskis Country, within an hour's drive of Calgary. Summer visitors come here to picnic and fish along the river, watch for grazing sheep, hike on one of several short interpretive trails or simply marvel at the area's rugged beauty.

The road west from Turner Valley climbs through rolling foothills dotted with ranches and stands of aspen and spruce forest. Seventy years ago, large sections of these foothills were scarcely treed because of uncontrolled forest fires. These devastating fires nonetheless improved ungulate habitat by removing mature trees and stimulating new growth.

Cattle now graze the rolling grasslands, while beavers maintain dams on creeks, creating low wetlands. The dominant feature throughout is the Sheep River, which carves a deep channel through bedrock as it tumbles out of the low mountains and across the foothills.

A short distance past the Kananaskis Country boundary and visitor centre is the Sandy McNabb Campground. The 1.5-kilometre Sandy McNabb interpretive trail loops from a campground parking lot through open forest and willowy bogs to a viewpoint overlooking the Sheep River Valley. This terrace, carved by glacial meltwaters, stands about 100 metres above the Sheep River.

From its source on Mount Rae, the river descends 1,000 metres in elevation to its junction with the Highwood River. This steady descent has resulted in a series of small rapids that downstream are a whitewater kayaker's delight. Farther upstream, the river drops over a succession of sandstone ledges into exquisitely foaming pools.

Just beyond the campground is the eastern boundary of Sheep River Provincial Park, which includes a preserve for wintering bighorn sheep that have grazed here for more than 1,000 years. A short trail from the nearby Bighorn day-use area leads to a viewpoint overlooking an expanse of meadows and slopes frequented by sheep.

Swept clear much of the winter by chinook winds, these grasslands provide critical habitat for a herd of about 150 bighorn sheep. But some sheep are now staying in the sanctuary throughout the year, rather than migrating up the valley to much larger summer ranges. This has resulted in overgrazing and crowding and, consequently, a greater incidence of parasitic lungworm infections. To help preserve wildlife habitat and to connect migration routes, two additional area parks have been created—Bluerock Wildland Provincial Park and Elbow-Sheep Wildland Park.

Near the end of the road is Bluerock Campground. A 2-kilometre interpretive loop climbs steadily from the campground along Bluerock Creek to the site of an old sawmill. The grassy, flower-covered hillside on the right contrasts sharply with the mossy forest on the steep opposite bank. The latter is sheltered from sun and wind and thus retains its moisture.

A sawmill operated briefly here in the 1940s under the stewardship of Napp Lefavre. Many such logging camps suffered from poor markets and difficulties in hauling timber out of the valley on steep, narrow roads. Rusty bolts, bits of boards and an old bridge in the grassy clearing below are all that remain of Lefavre's abandoned sawmill.

Across the valley in Junction Creek, John Lineman established one of several logging camps at the turn of the century. The logs were floated down the river to his mill in Okotoks, an often treacherous operation that claimed a number of lives. Forest fires, not poor markets, halted his activities here in 1910.

While the Sheep Valley's resources of timber, coal and oil were keenly sought, the rugged terrain, along with market vagaries, outlasted all entrepreneurs. For example, Pat Burns, a wealthy Calgarian, opened a coal mine in 1913 but the expected Calgary and Southern Railway was never built into this valley. Instead, the coal was hauled out by wagon until the mine closed in 1923. Today, the only enduring form of human activity in these upper reaches is the pilgrimage of nature-loving visitors.

Highwood Pass Loop

ROUTE: From its intersection with Macleod Trail/Highway 2, at the south end of Calgary, take Highway 22X west for 17 kilometres. Drive south on Highway 22 for 49 kilometres to Longview and then west on Highway 541 for 44 kilometres to the Highwood Junction. Turn north on Highway 40, which is followed over Highwood Pass for 105 kilometres to the Trans-Canada Highway. Head east for 61 kilometres to reach Canada Olympic Park at the west edge of Calgary.
DRIVING DISTANCE: About 275 kilometres return.
NOTE: Highway 40 from Highwood Junction to the Kananaskis Trail Junction is closed from December 1 to June 15 to protect wintering herds of bighorn sheep.

This is one of the finest and most diversified driving tours in Canada. It journeys through the heart of southern Alberta's ranching country and then climbs past forested foothills and folded mountains to cross the highest drivable pass in Canada. From this lofty spot, one can take a superb alpine hike or a shorter interpretive walk.

The trip begins by passing through the rolling landscape southwest of Calgary. This is ranching country, ranging from the splendid stables and show-jumping grounds of Spruce Meadows to foothills spreads that have been producing some of Canada's finest beef for more than a century. This is also prime real estate, commanding high prices for suburban acreages that offer short commutes and spectacular scenery. For the passing motorist, the foothill and mountain vistas seem to improve over every rise en route to Longview.

The route heads west at the outskirts of Longview, a village of 300 people that serves the ranching and petroleum industries. Area oil discoveries in 1936 sparked a boom, prompting the sudden emergence of Little New York and Little Chicago, each with an instant population of more than 1,500. The discovery of oil at Leduc in 1947 signalled the end of Little

Chicago but Little New York, earlier renamed Longview, still survives on a much smaller scale.

In these foothills, cattle grazing extends up the Highwood Valley well into Kananaskis Country, as is evident by cows, and their deposits, on the road. Since the late 1800s, ranchers have been moving their herds in spring along the flat river terraces to the high country, where the cattle graze on grassy slopes until fall. The cattle drives follow the same trails up the Highwood Valley as those used by the Stoney Indians, explorers, and, later, coal prospectors and loggers.

The Highwood Valley also provides a migration corridor and critical habitat for wildlife. In winter, warm chinook winds sweep the snow off open slopes, allowing elk, bighorn sheep and deer to feed on exposed grasses. While much elk habitat has elsewhere been destroyed, undisturbed grassy slopes in the Highwood Valley are able to sustain a group of 600 animals, the largest herd in Kananaskis Country. The valley's upper reaches also support small populations of such threatened predators as cougars, wolverines, wolves and grizzly bears.

North of Highwood Junction, Highway 40 begins a steady climb between the Elk Range on the left and the Misty Range on the right. George Dawson named the latter for the inclement weather shrouding the peaks during his geological explorations of the mid-1880s.

Notice the exaggerated folding on the faces of some of these mountains. This wavy appearance was caused during mountain building between 80 million and 40 million years ago, when land forces from the west caused horizontal layers here to be folded and fractured.

The climb levels off at the summit of Highwood Pass, which at 2,206 metres is the highest paved road in Canada. The pass was used for thousands of years by aboriginal peoples and, later, by fur traders and explorers as a means of moving between the Highwood and Kananaskis valleys.

Hiker on the Ptarmigan Cirque trail near Highwood Pass.

Here, you can step from the car and immediately be surrounded by wildflowers in a subalpine meadow near the tree
line. This is a fascinating and harsh landscape, where the
growing season is compressed into less than three months
and trees take hundreds of years to reach a modest height,
despite an annual precipitation of some 200 centimetres.

The lofty elevation here, near the Continental Divide, has
also been a biological blessing. The sudden change in the
slope angle along the Elk Range to the northeast marks the
high point reached by scouring ice during glaciation. In the
higher, ice-free areas, called nunataks, unique alpine grasses
and rock crawlers, ancient ancestors of today's grasshopper,
survived the ice age. The diversity of vegetation here is also
enhanced by the absence in the underlying bedrock of calci-
um-rich limestone, which limits the growth of many subalpine plants.

To learn more about this landscape, take the Highwood
Meadows interpretive trail, a 500-metre walk from the

Highwood Pass parking lot. The trail is on a boardwalk, built to protect the fragile soils and plants from the damaging impact of foot traffic. Despite their diminutive stature, some of the larch and fir trees along the trail are more than 350 years old.

Across the highway is the Ptarmigan Cirque trail, one of the finest short hikes in the Rockies and a quick approach to alpine terrain. The 2.5-kilometre trail initially climbs steeply as it passes through mature stands of alpine fir, Engelmann spruce and subalpine larch. But after a kilometre, it quickly levels out into a sublime alpine meadow, which in summer is covered in wildflowers and ground-hugging plants that make the most of the short growing season.

At this elevation, it might seem strange to see fossilized marine life such as horned corals in the rocks. The corals, once growing in an inland sea, were preserved in sedimentary rocks that were thrust to these heights during the process of mountain building. Those tremendous forces are clearly visible in the folded rocks and vertical bedding planes of nearby Mount Arethusa.

Ptarmigan Cirque is named for the hardy white-tailed ptarmigan that live here year-round. Their speckled coats, which blend into the rocky landscape, turn white in the fall to match the winter snow cover. The cirque was formed by mountain glaciers that carved the bowl shape. Just before "stop eight" on the interpretive trail, a well-beaten path leads through scree to gain the rubbly top of a moraine, left by the retreating glacier. From here, you can gaze up at the barren bowl protected by Mount Rae, the highest peak in the area.

Back in the car, the descent is swift and steady from Highwood Pass into the Kananaskis Valley. Just beyond the pass is another short interpretive walk, the Rock Glacier, so called because the jumbled rocks move in a similar manner to an advancing ice glacier. More impressive rock is found farther along on the right, where the limestone faces of, successively,

Mount Elpoca and Mount Wintour have been severely weathered into a jagged appearance.

A few kilometres beyond Highwood Pass is a 1-kilometre trail that leads to Elbow Lake, a pleasant destination for a short hike and picnic. Above the lake, the small glacier on the north face of Mount Rae is the principal source of the Elbow River, which provides Calgary with nearly half its drinking water.

The road levels out as it proceeds north up the Kananaskis Valley. The relative quiet of Highwood Pass, protected within Peter Lougheed Provincial Park, is replaced in this busy valley by such recreational facilities as stocked trout ponds, a recreational vehicle park, numerous campgrounds, an alpine village, two golf courses and a ski resort. For more information, see the Kananaskis Valley trip description on pages 185-190.

Bar U Ranch National Historic Site

ROUTE: From its intersection with Macleod Trail/Highway 2 at the south end of Calgary, take Highway 22X west for 17 kilometres. Drive about 60 kilometres south on Highway 22 past Longview to the signed Bar U Ranch turnoff to the west.

DRIVING DISTANCE: About 80 kilometres one way.

NOTE: The historic site is open daily 10:00 a.m. to 6:00 p.m. from mid-May to mid-October. Admission charged. Phone 1-800-568-4996 or (403) 395-2212.

The golden era of the 100,000-acre (40,470-hectare) ranches in Alberta's foothills is long gone. But this century-old story lives on at the Bar U Ranch National Historic Site, where remnants of one of the earliest and most enduring of these massive spreads have been preserved. There, interpreters dressed in jeans and cowboy hats walk visitors through historic ranch buildings in the process of being restored.

The Bar U was one of the four big southern Alberta ranches that emerged from the Dominion Lands Act of 1881, which allowed wealthy eastern investors to lease up to 100,000 acres of rangeland for one cent per acre. These business people included the Allan family of Montreal, which teamed up with Quebec stockman Fred Stimson to form the North West Cattle Company, better known for its Bar U brand.

Riding in grass up to his horse's belly, Stimson arrived in 1881 at the site of the Bar U Ranch, along the banks of Pekisko Creek. A year later, the federal lease was granted and 3,000 head of Durham shorthorn cattle were trailed up from Idaho. By the end of the decade, the Bar U had grown to nearly 158,000 acres (63,940 hectares), with more than 10,000 cattle, 800 horses, and enough people to make it the largest settlement between Calgary and Fort Macleod. (In 1891, the ranch population included a horse breaker named Harry Longabaugh, better known as the Sundance Kid.) Cattle were sold for domestic consumption and to markets as far afield as England.

Historic buildings under restoration at Bar U Ranch.

Besides vast expanses of cheap land, the early foothills cattlemen were blessed by sufficient rainfall and, in winter, sheltering coulees and warming chinook winds that exposed the rough fescue grasses. Called the queen of grasses, in part because the base of its barbed blades is a royal purple, rough fescue provided bountiful winter protein if not overgrazed.

But winter was not always benign. Foothills ranchers suffered terrible losses in 1886-87 and in 1906-07—16,000 imported Mexican cattle perished on the Bar U alone in the latter winter—forcing those who survived to invest in fencing and haying. By then, railway lines, irrigation ditches and the growing pressure of farming were already carving up the open range. The North West Cattle Company had taken advantage of an 1892 provision allowing ranchers to buy up to 10 per cent of their leased lands for $1.25 an acre. It thus owned 15,000 acres (6,070 hectares) in addition to leased lands.

In 1902, the Bar U was sold for $220,000 to a group that included its one-time foreman, George Lane. He soon began importing French purebred Percherons, which were bred for sale to area settlers as draft horses and which won numerous international awards. During Lane's reign, the Prince of Wales came for a visit and later bought the EP Ranch, which still operates under local ownership just west of the Bar U. Following Lane's death in 1925, the Bar U was sold to cattle and meat-packing baron Pat Burns, who was then said to be able to ride from Calgary to the U.S. border without once leaving his property. Under the Burns family stewardship, the ranch introduced modern technology, increased its grain acreage, and replaced the shorthorn cattle with more durable Herefords.

In 1950, the Bar U's original holdings were split up and sold to area ranchers, ending a storied era. Four decades later, part of the ranch returned to its original grantor when Parks Canada acquired 367 acres (145 hectares) of the original headquarters and some surrounding rangeland to create a national historic site commemorating the evolution of Canada's ranching industry.

The site has a new orientation centre, where visitors can tour exhibits, watch a video, sample authentic ranch food and browse through a general store. Heading outside, it's easy to spend a couple of hours touring the 35 historic structures that include an 1882 saddle horse barn, a cookhouse, blacksmith and harness repair shops, and a Percheron barn. Many of these buildings are slowly being restored. From spring to fall, there are special events, such as roping and branding demonstrations and heavy horse displays. Parks Canada also offers a public archaeology program, whereby participants can help literally unearth the site's ranching history.

Nanton and Chain Lakes Provincial Park

ROUTE: From the Highway 22X overpass, drive 68 kilometres south on Highway 2 to Nanton. To reach Chain Lakes Provincial Park, take Secondary 533, from the southern outskirts of Nanton, for 38 kilometres west to its intersection with Highway 22 and the park entrance. Return to Calgary by driving 25 kilometres north on Highway 22, 31 kilometres east on Secondary 540, and north on Highway 2A to regain Highway 2 near High River.
DRIVING DISTANCE: About 220 kilometres return.

This lovely tour rises from the prairie flats through exquisitely rolling hills to Chain Lakes Provincial Park, a popular destination for fishing and picnicking. Along the way, you can test Alberta's version of a magnetic hill.

Little of the countryside along this trip is still natural. The prairies en route to Nanton are ploughed and often irrigated, the hills dotted with grazing cattle, and the Chain Lakes are dammed and stocked with trout. Yet the landscape, with its undulating topography and mountain views, retains a bucolic charm largely undiminished by human activities.

Contrary to first impressions, there is more to Nanton than twin strips of highway flanked by businesses catering to the motorist. Away from the double-lane asphalt, this is one of the more pleasant small communities south of Calgary. Nanton is perhaps best known for its pure spring water, which can be sampled from a tap along northbound Highway 2 near the old one-room MacEwan Schoolhouse. Nanton spring water is also bottled by a local company and sold to distant markets.

While in town, it's worth visiting the Nanton Lancaster Society Air Museum (see pages 32-34) and strolling along the downtown Antique and Art Walk, which features shops housed in restored heritage buildings.

The route west from Nanton is one of the finest short drives in southern Alberta. It passes over the northern section of the Porcupine Hills, which separates the parallel valleys that contain Highways 2 and 22.

Just west of Nanton, the road crosses the old Macleod Trail, a north-south route that once extended from Fort Edmonton to Fort Benton in Montana. The route was used for centuries by aboriginal peoples, early white traders, nineteenth-century cattle drivers and North-West Mounted Police patrols. Though the fences of homesteaders cut the route off after 1900, vestiges of the deep wagon ruts can still be seen in farmers' fields.

Where the road bends south just before an abrupt rise of hills, it's worth taking a short detour by continuing west for a couple of kilometres. Along the north side of a narrow valley are some fine examples of sandstone outcrops. Back on Secondary 533, the road passes through an impressive line of hills cut by a network of ravines or coulees.

At 24 kilometres from Highway 2, a short road leads to an advertised "magnetic hill," where a car in neutral will provide a mild sensation of coasting uphill. The real highlight is at the end of this road, where a lookout affords a magnificent view across the creased hills to the prairie expanse. A plaque here commemorates ranching pioneer and Calgary entrepreneur A.E. Cross, whose descendants still own considerable ranchlands in the area.

The same success was not enjoyed by the Oxley Ranche, which held extensive lands along nearby Willow Creek. Formed in 1882 as one of the four big ranches in southern Alberta, the Oxley suffered from internal squabbling between its manager and aristocratic shareholders in Britain. Reorganized once, it was sold in 1903.

The final stretch of highway, on a good gravel surface, follows Willow Creek, which meanders, appropriately enough, through thickets of willows. Despite its diminutive size, the creek is a major water source, meeting the needs of irrigation farmers and the towns of Claresholm and Granum to the southeast. Its small but steady flow is assured by a nearby dam that backs the creek's flow into Chain Lakes Reservoir, formerly a series of shallow, spring-fed lakes from which the name is derived.

Completed in the mid-1960s, the long, narrow reservoir initiated the creation several years later of Chain Lakes Provincial Park. The park is an interesting blend of ecosystems, where fescue grasses and prairie crocuses can be found alongside higher-elevation species like western wood lily and mountain fleabane. A marsh below the dam is home to a diversity of wetland plants as well as great blue herons, common loons, warblers and shorebirds.

Historically, the valley bottom here was used for grazing cattle and growing substantial hay crops. Visitors today can see an interesting collection of munching horses, cows and sheep, used as a management tool to reduce an escalating fire hazard. Controlled burns are also being employed to remove old grasses and willows and allow new growth that will feed the area's moose and elk.

The park is a pleasant place to have a lakeside picnic, take a short stroll, or simply admire the views of the nearby Livingstone Range. But it is most popular as a place to fish for stocked rainbow trout, which can reach sizes of more than three kilograms. It's not unusual to see a considerable number of anglers casting into the murky waters from shore or boats or, in winter, dangling a baited hook through a hole in the ice.

Return to Calgary by heading north and then taking Secondary 540 east toward Highway 2A. This is a quiet and highly scenic route, offering superb views of the mountains and of the amazingly deep valley of Pekisko Creek as it angles northeast to join the Highwood River.

Aerospace Tour

ROUTE: From the Highway 22X overpass, drive 68 kilometres south on Highway 2 to Nanton. From Nanton, go 29 kilometres east on Secondary 533 and then 2.5 kilometres south and east to the RCAF Vulcan Aerodrome. It's another 13 kilometres east and north on mostly gravel roads to reach Vulcan. The return to Calgary, via your choice of primary and secondary highways, is about 100 kilometres.

DRIVING DISTANCE: About 215 kilometres return.

NOTE: The Nanton Lancaster Society Air Museum is open 9:00 a.m. to 5:00 p.m. daily from May 1 to October 31, and 10:00 a.m. to 4:00 p.m. on weekends the rest of the year. Phone (403) 646-2270. The Vulcan Tourism and Trek Station is open daily from late May to early September and from Monday to Friday the rest of the year. Phone (403) 485-2994.

What do World War II bombers and science fiction spaceships have in common with small-town southern Alberta? More than you might think. In this back-to-the-future aerospace tour, you can crawl through the fuselage of a hulking Lancaster bomber, stare at the prairie ruins of a World War II air training school and visit a town dedicated to the space age trappings of the television show *Star Trek*.

A Vulcan mural reflects town interests that range from ranching to bombers and rockets.

The tour begins with a drive south to Nanton, a charming prairie town and home of the Nanton Lancaster Society Air Museum. The museum opened in 1992 to honour the Canadian and British flyers who served in the dangerous Bomber Command during World War II; more than 10,000 Canadians died in the aerial battle over Europe. It also pays tribute to the southern Alberta communities that provided bases for training Commonwealth pilots during the war.

The museum's 637 square metres of display space houses an impressive collection of period airplanes, including a Blenheim bomber, a Fleet Fawn and a Tiger Moth. The showpiece is a restored Lancaster bomber, the Canadian-made workhorse of Bomber Command. Visitors can squeeze through the sparse and narrow fuselage and imagine flying this defenseless black monster on bombing missions into enemy territory, protected only by speed and darkness.

More than 7,000 Lancasters were built during World War II. Fewer than 15 remain intact worldwide. The bomber on display in Nanton nearly shared the same fate, vandalized and rusting away in a farmer's field near Vulcan after being retired from activity duty in 1959. Several enterprising locals rescued the Lancaster and hauled it across fields to Nanton, where it continued to deteriorate for 25 years until a restoration and museum plan was finally hatched.

From Nanton, the aerospace tour heads east on Secondary 533 through level farmland. Just after crossing the Little Bow River, the main road bends north to become Secondary 804. Instead, continue east on slightly rougher pavement and then follow the signs south and east to reach the strange sight of half a dozen large, dilapidated buildings on the bald prairie, overlooking the Little Bow Valley.

The skeletons of these hangars and grass-infested runways are all that remain of the RCAF Vulcan Aerodrome, where, during World War II, more than 1,000 Allied students received flight training at one of many Canadian schools under the British Commonwealth Air Training Plan. Tutored to fly the twin-engine Anson II aircraft, graduates from the Vulcan school were destined for Bomber Command in England.

From the aerodrome, head northeast on good gravel roads to Vulcan, which housed most of these wartime pilot trainees. Today, Vulcan's aerial interests are firmly focused on the fictitious future. In the early 1990s, the town tied its tourism fortunes to the fictitious planet of Vulcan, the home of Mr. Spock in the long-running TV show *Star Trek*. Soon thereafter, businesses on Vulcan's main street began sporting window paintings of the sharp-eared Spock and other crew members. Things really got serious in the late 1990s with the construction of a 9.5-metre-long replica starship, loosely based on the *USS Enterprise*, and a space station that now houses the town's tourism office and sells *Star Trek* memorabilia, including clothing.

Not all of Vulcan's passion for outer space is based on fantasy. In 1962, a 20-kilogram meteorite believed to be from the Mars-Jupiter asteroid belt was found in a field near Vulcan. Now, a local astronomical society hopes to build a public observatory 8 kilometres west of Vulcan atop an 1,100-metre hill, taking advantage of the dark, unobstructed prairie skies. Perhaps its telescope might one day spot a passing spaceship.

Willow Creek Provincial Park

ROUTE: From the Highway 22X overpass, drive 92 kilometres south on Highway 2. Turn right on Secondary 527 west, which is followed for 15.5 kilometres to Willow Creek Provincial Park.
DRIVING DISTANCE: About 110 kilometres one way.

Willow Creek Provincial Park is a small prairie jewel tucked away in a sheltered valley beneath the Porcupine Hills. The lovely drive and shaded creek make this an excellent destination for an afternoon picnic and stroll. A return stopover in historic High River is also included in the itinerary.

The approach from Calgary provides no clue of what lies ahead. The prairie terrain is mainly level, relieved only by the distant rise of western foothills and mountains. Secondary 527 angles southwest toward these hills and away from the busy Highway 2.

At 5 kilometres along 527, the road crosses the old Macleod Trail, the north-south route used by travellers for centuries before the arrival of the railway. In some places, traces of wagon ruts can still be seen among the prairie grasses and farmlands.

The road becomes more enchanting with each passing kilometre, as it dips through grassy draws grazed by cows and passes beneath foothill ridges studded with sandstone outcrops. Where the road swings south, it's tempting to continue endlessly west on gravel roads that climb through rolling ranchland into the Porcupine Hills. After all, the most inter-

Looking northwest from Willow Creek Provincial Park.

esting trips are usually spontaneous explorations off the beaten track.

Soon enough, the road reaches Willow Creek Provincial Park. The 109-hectare park is situated in a large valley that was once a runoff channel for a glacial lake. The lake was created when glacial meltwaters from the mountains backed up against the continental ice sheet. When the ice sheet retreated, the lake drained.

Today, the park is an oasis in the otherwise dry prairie. The sheltered valley is fed by Willow Creek, creating a rich and diverse habitat. The moist flood plain supports stands of balsam poplar, black cottonwood and narrow leaf cottonwood, the last not commonly found in Alberta. The shaded creek attracts populations of mule and white-tailed deer, beavers, coyotes, weasels and occasionally moose.

This lush environment is in stark contrast to the dry grasslands on the bench above the creek, where rough fescues, other native grasses, and sagebrush predominate. On one terrace near the park bridge, an aboriginal tipi ring has been preserved. The ring of rocks, once used to hold down a skin tipi, was left when the camp was moved. A buffalo jump and a major hunting camp are located just east of the park.

Blackfoot, Peigan and Blood Indians were attracted to this valley by the buffalo, berries and winter shelter it offered. They also considered the cottonwoods, which grew along the flood plain, sacred.

White residents, particularly from the nearby town of Stavely, were attracted to this site for recreation. They picnicked along the creek and held dances in a hall constructed on an old sawmill loading platform. The dance hall was damaged beyond repair when Willow Creek flooded in 1963. Such floods have been subsequently prevented by construction upstream of the dam that created Chain Lakes Reservoir.

Willow Creek Provincial Park, created in 1957, still attracts picnickers and nature lovers. Birdwatchers often flock to the area to look for great blue herons, belted kingfishers, northern orioles, meadow larks, kestrels and cliff swallows, which nest along the steep creek banks.

On the return trip, it's worth taking a detour on Highway 2A from north of Nanton to the historic town of High River. The Blackfoot name for the Highwood River is *Ispitsi*, for the tall cottonwood trees that grew along its banks. A portion of one ancient and sacred cottonwood, the Medicine Tree, has been preserved among the living trees within George Lane Memorial Park in central High River. In 1800, explorer David Thompson camped near here along the river.

In 1869, Americans Dave Akers and "Liver Eating" Johnston built the nearby Spitzee Post to trade whisky to native people in exchange for buffalo hides and furs. This and two subsequent posts were short-lived. By the mid-1870s, the North-West Mounted Police had shut down the illegal whisky trade in present-day southern Alberta.

With the signing of the Indian treaties in 1877, the land around High River became available for ranching. One of southern Alberta's four big early ranches, the North-West

Cattle Company, was formed west along the Highwood River in 1882. Better known by its brand, Bar U, the ranch prospered under the management of Fred Stimson. It eventually was acquired by a former employee, George Lane, one of the founders of the Calgary Stampede. Bar U is gradually being restored as a historic site, and is open to the public May to October. (See pages 26-29.)

Visitors to High River can learn more about the town's history by visiting the Museum of the Highwood, housed in the town's original sandstone train station. A walking tour through downtown reveals the area's history through huge murals painted on building walls. The town is also the birthplace of former Canadian prime minister Joe Clark.

Claresholm-Porcupine Hills

ROUTE: From the Highway 22X overpass, drive 108 kilometres south on Highway 2 to Claresholm. Head west on Secondary 520 over the Porcupine Hills to Highway 22, and follow it north back toward Calgary.
DRIVING DISTANCE: About 300 kilometres return.
NOTE: The Claresholm Museum is open daily 9:30 a.m. to 5:30 p.m. from late May to early September. Phone (403) 625-3131.

The Porcupine Hills are an unusual rise of land in southwest Alberta that at their crest have never been covered by glacial ice. This fine day trip climbs to the height of these hills and offers a short hike to a stunning viewpoint. En route, there is a short stopover in Claresholm.

The approach from Calgary follows Highway 2 through gently rolling prairie, intermittently bisected by the small valleys of the Sheep and Highwood rivers and smaller drainages. To the west, the forested Porcupine Hills parallel much of the highway, rising to their height southwest of Claresholm.

Although the old Macleod Trail passed through the area, it

was the southward extension of the Calgary and Edmonton Railway in 1891 that put Claresholm on the map. Named by the railway, Claresholm was located in a low spot, where collected water could feed the steam engines and railway cars would not roll away.

In 1902, O.J. Amundsen had the townsite surveyed and convinced 25 settlers from North Dakota to move here. Surrounded by good agricultural land, the town quickly grew. By 1910, a row of wood frame buildings lined the main street along the railway line. Visitors today can take a self-guided walking tour of downtown buildings from this era and from subsequent booms. A tour map is available in the visitor information centre, located in the Claresholm Museum.

The museum is housed in Claresholm's architectural jewel, the old sandstone train station. The building was originally part of a larger station built in 1886 and located on 9th Avenue in Calgary. When that station was being replaced, it was split in two, with one section going to Claresholm and the other to High River, where they were reconstructed around 1910. The station was converted to a museum in 1969, a year after the passenger train service was halted.

A lovely garden in front of the station honours Louise McKinney, a prominent local politician, temperance promoter and religious activist in the Methodist Church. In the 1917 provincial election, she ran successfully for the agrarian Non-Partisan League, becoming one of the first two women elected to a Canadian legislature. She was also one of five women in the famous Persons Case, which in 1929 established women as "persons" who could hold office as Canadian senators.

West of Claresholm, Secondary 520 soon crosses Willow Creek. An upstream dam on the creek at Chain Lakes Reservoir provides a steady supply of water to Claresholm, Granum and area irrigation farmers. Within 15 kilometres, the road begins to climb into the Porcupine Hills, cut by coulees and dotted with ranches. The name Porcupine Hills refers to a Blackfoot description of the spiny, tree-lined ridges that resemble a porcupine in profile.

During glacial advances, continental ice sheets flowed around much of this area, leaving these high hills standing above the prairies. In fact, the height of the Porcupine Hills is one of the few areas in Alberta untouched by glaciation. At the end of the last ice age, the draining of the glaciated valley to the west carved a channel that separated the Porcupine Hills from the foothills.

The Porcupine Hills were not totally untouched by glaciation. On their lower eastern slopes, for example, sizable meltwater channels were formed against the edge of the receding continental ice sheet. When the ice melted, these channels, running at a level elevation along the side of the hills, were left high and dry above the valley floor. One such channel, called the Canyon, can be seen west of Claresholm.

Geologically, it could be argued that the Porcupine Hills are not part of the foothills. While the foothills exhibit the same subsurface folding and thrust faulting as the mountains, the beds of sandstone and shale that underlie the Porcupine Hills dip gently, in the manner of the plains to the east.

Where the Porcupine Hills reach their height along Secondary 520, drive 1.8 kilometres south on the Skyline Road. Park at a low point in the road, cross a fence to the west and hike north on a rough track that parallels the fence line. Close any gates you open as this walk is on a Crown-owned grazing lease. Within a kilometre, a hilltop dotted with immense old Douglas firs is reached. The main ridge of the Porcupine Hills, with its considerable variation in elevation and topography, contains ecosystems of the montane, sub-alpine and boreal forests as well as those of the aspen parkland and prairie grassland.

This lofty perch provides exceptional views west to the Livingstone and High Rock ranges. Below is Happy Valley, which contains Highway 22 and grazing cattle. These lush lands are part of the Waldron Grazing Co-op, a syndicate of ranchers that, in misspelled name, carries on the tradition of the famous Walrond Ranche.

Created in 1883, the Walrond was one of the four big ranches that briefly ruled southern Alberta. Named after its principal investor, Sir John Walrond of Britain, the ranch was at first a prosperous undertaking along the northern reaches of the Oldman River. But following a severe winter that ended in 1907, the herd was sold and its lease relinquished. More recently, many of its former lands have been acquired by the co-op. The 1894 Walrond Ranche House was moved in the 1980s to the Pincher Creek Museum, where it can be viewed today.

From this height of land, Secondary 520 descends quickly to reach Highway 22, the return route north to Calgary. West of this junction is the Whaleback, a long, heavily treed ridge that parallels the highway for some distance. The Whaleback contains Alberta's largest and most undisturbed area of montane landscape, characterized here by open forests and grasslands and frequented by elk and deer. A portion of the Whaleback Ridge is protected within the Upper Bob Creek Ecological Reserve, to the southwest. (See pages 45-48.)

Foothills Tour

ROUTE: From its intersection with Highway 2 south, drive west for 17 kilometres on Highway 22X and 77 kilometres south on Highway 22. Just north of Chain Lakes Reservoir, turn west on Secondary 532, and follow it for 26 kilometres to its junction with Secondary 940, the Forestry Trunk Road. Drive 39 kilometres south on 940 and then 22 kilometres east on Secondary 517 to rejoin Highway 22 and follow it north to Calgary.

DRIVING DISTANCE: About 320 kilometres return.

NOTE: Secondary 532 west from Chain Lakes is a fairly rough gravel road that adds, I feel, a rugged dimension to the trip. It is certainly passable by passenger vehicles when reasonably dry. This section can be avoided by taking paved Secondary 541 west from Longview and then heading south on 940, the Forestry Trunk Road.

The Calgary area is celebrated for its mountains, prairies and low rolling ranchlands. All are thinly treed, allowing for the distant vistas for which southern Alberta is famous. For a change of pace, how about a trip that celebrates the heavier forests of its foothills and lower mountain slopes? This trip rises over the rugged foothills of southern Alberta and then follows the Oldman River out of the heavy forests and back onto the edge of the plains. Along the way there's a stop at the lovely Livingstone Falls.

The drive south from Calgary roughly follows the eastern edge of southern Alberta's foothills, a thin belt that parallels the Rocky Mountains on a northwest-southeast alignment. Indeed, Highway 22 south of Longview marks the geological boundary between the foothills formations to the west and the plains to the east.

Driving cattle on Highway 22.

While both are underlain by sedimentary layers of primarily sandstones and shales, the plains strata have remained fairly horizontal. The foothills structures, by contrast, were shaped some 50 million years ago by the same forces that earlier created the mountains to the west. Their layers have thus been intricately thrust faulted and folded, causing older rocks to be stacked on top of younger ones.

Drilling for natural gas and oil in the Turner Valley field has revealed highly complex rock structures beneath the surface. Clues to these underground structures can often be found along riverbanks where the bedrock has been exposed. The north bank of the Highwood River near Longview is a good place to look for these features.

The reason these complex structures are not revealed at the surface is the bedrock of sandstones and shales is fairly soft and has been eroded over the years into the gentler slopes of the foothills. Sandstone, however, is more resistant than shale and forms the parallel ridges one finds in the foothills. Where exposed as outcrops, these sandstone ridges are called hogbacks. The dips or valleys between these ridges are generally underlain by softer shales.

Just north of Chain Lakes Reservoir, the route swings west to climb through the foothills and into the front ranges of the Rockies. The road initially follows the headwaters of Willow Creek and then commences a roller-coaster ride through aspen forest that soon gives way to pine and spruce.

Higher up, the valley walls become more steep-sided and several drainages descend from a rockier ridge, the first evidence of a transition to a mountain environment. The road climbs steeply to a divide that provides superb views back down the valley and over the contorted hills to flatter lands beyond. To the near west is Plateau Mountain, a flat-topped peak that escaped the last period of glaciation and, likely as a result, has unusual patterns of rocks on its surface.

From this height of land, the road descends quickly into

heavier coniferous forest, a fairly steady companion the length of the Forestry Trunk Road. Ten kilometres south on this road, it's well worth stopping for a picnic or stroll at the Livingstone Falls Campground, set amid well-spaced trees. The river here and the mountain range to the east are named for the famous African explorer and missionary David Livingstone.

Although small in size, Livingstone Falls are unique. A rock ledge has been thrust up into the current, allowing the water to slide elegantly down its surface, rather than falling off it. The tiny river divides into two channels here, forming closely spaced waterfalls over the same ledge.

Beyond the campground, the road soon follows the Oldman River, which tumbles out of mountains to the west and heads south along this valley. The river's name comes from a Blackfoot word that means "the river the Old Man played upon." According to legend, the Blackfoot god Old Man Napi created a playing field near where the river is joined by the tributary Livingstone River.

The Oldman River suddenly swings east through the Livingstone Range at a spectacular canyon known as the Gap. The route follows the canyon east along Secondary 517. This slash in the mountain flank is believed to have been initially carved by an ancient Oldman River and subsequently enlarged by glaciation. In much more recent times, the Gap has also been an important transportation corridor for moving cattle to and from summer ranges in the high country.

Beyond the Gap, the road suddenly emerges into rolling hills that are largely naked. There are, however, patches of aspen in sheltered spots and thick stands of Douglas fir on slopes to the south. The lower foothills south of the Bow River are actually a southern extension of aspen parkland, more commonly found in central Alberta. This ecosystem is dominated by a mixture of aspen forest and prairie grassland.

Whaleback

ROUTE: Perhaps the most direct route is to drive, from the Highway 22X overpass, 68 kilometres south on Highway 2 to Nanton. From the south end of town, go 38 kilometres west on Secondary 533 to Highway 22 and then 30 kilometres south to a small pull-off on the right (it's just under 4 kilometres south of the Secondary 520 junction). Park beside a gate, beyond which a rocky track ascends a hill to the west.

DRIVING DISTANCE: About 140 kilometres one way.

NOTE: Hiking time is about four to five hours return, 375 metres elevation gain. To reach the Whaleback, you must cross private and then leased Crown land. Unless you have written consent (phone 403-625-2348) to drive onto the Waldron Grazing Co-operative's land, you must park at the highway and proceed on foot (it only adds a couple of kilometres) sticking to existing tracks wherever possible and taking care not to disturb grazing cattle. If visitors fail to follow these simple rules, this easy public access will be lost.

From spring through fall, it's well worth visiting this unique foothills landscape in the midst of southwestern Alberta's rolling cattle country. This trip describes a half-day excursion—wear sturdy hiking footwear—along the northern portion of Whaleback Ridge. From this lofty perch, surrounded by stands of ancient Douglas fir and gnarled limber pine, you can gaze across sheltered valleys and smaller ridges to the nearby peaks of the Livingstone Range.

The Whaleback—named for its series of spine-like ridges—boasts Canada's largest and healthiest montane landscape, which is characterized by a relatively dry climate and a patchwork of grassy slopes and dense forest. A rare environment in Alberta, the montane is most commonly found in mountain valleys, such as along the Bow River in Banff National Park, where it has been largely carved up by roads, railways and commercial development.

At 235 square kilometres, the roadless Whaleback remains

largely intact. Its mix of open grass slopes, heavy timber and wetlands offers a rich habitat for elk, cougar, grizzly bears and wolves, eagles, songbirds and an abundance of wildflowers. It also harbours magnificent stands of Douglas fir and, on exposed upper slopes and ridges, limber pine bent by centuries of chinook winds.

In mid-1999, the Alberta government granted the Whaleback full environmental protection under its Special Places 2000 program. As a wildland, most of the Whaleback will be off-limits to new roads, logging, mining and recreational development. This protection became possible when Amoco Canada Petroleum surrendered area leases to the Nature Conservancy of Canada.

From the highway, the route begins by ascending a short hill and passing a large pond frequented by watering cattle. These lands were once part of the vast cattle empire of the

Looking west from Whaleback Ridge across Bob Creek Valley to the Livingstone Ridge.

Walrond Ranche, formed in 1883 and prosperous until winter blizzards hastened its demise in the early 1900s. Much of its original property was acquired in the 1960s by the Waldron Grazing Co-operative, a syndicate of ranchers which owns or leases most of the southern half of Whaleback Ridge. During the summer, the Whaleback area is grazed by several thousand cattle, most of them yearling steers castrated as calves. Visitors perturbed by the wanderings and droppings of these animals should consider that area ranchers have, by lightly grazing their cattle on the rough fescue grasses over the decades, helped keep this spectacular landscape intact.

The track soon cuts through the thickly wooded lower slopes of Black Mountain, offering views back east to the Porcupine Hills and the first good look ahead to Whaleback Ridge. The undulating ridge is 30 kilometres long, with open, grassy slopes in the south giving way to denser forests of Douglas fir, white spruce, aspen and limber pine to the north. This mixture of exposed grasses and sheltering woods provides critical wintering habitat for about 2,000 elk, the second-largest herd in southern Alberta.

The route continues straight ahead, bypassing a track leading south. Just beyond, where the road turns north, step across a tiny creek and work your way northwest towards a prominent coulee, sticking to trails where you can find them. En route, you will pass beneath a controversial power line, erected in the 1980s, and skirt a small wetland that harbours a diversity of nesting songbirds. Beyond, follow a trail up the coulee until you can angle right up the final grassy slopes to the ridge.

The view that awaits is stunning—the Bob Creek Valley below and a succession of ridges rising to the front ranges of the Rocky Mountains. On the far side of Bob Creek is Little Whaleback Ridge, near where the sour gas well and access road were proposed. In the skies above, hawks and occasionally golden eagles can be seen riding the thermal currents.

As best as you can, follow the ridge line north, dropping down here and there to bypass narrow bits of fractured and exposed Belly River sandstone. Soon enough, you will reach a barbed wire fence marking the southern boundary of the small Bob Creek Ecological Reserve, which offers slightly greater protection than the rest of the Whaleback Ridge. From the reserve's edge, a rough road descends steeply into Breeders Valley, where a track leads south back to the approach route.

To explore the numerous other hikes in the area, consult *The Whaleback—A Walking Guide,* by Bob Blaxley (Calgary: Rocky Mountain Books, 1997).

Head-Smashed-In Buffalo Jump

ROUTE: From the Highway 22X overpass at Calgary's southern outskirts, drive 143 kilometres south on Highway 2. Follow the Head-Smashed-In Buffalo Jump signs west on Secondary 785 for 16 kilometres.

DRIVING DISTANCE: About 160 kilometres one way.

NOTE: The interpretive centre is open daily 9:00 a.m. to 6:00 p.m. from mid-May to mid-September, and 10:00 a.m. to 5:00 p.m. the rest of the year. Admission charged. For information or to book tours, phone (403) 553-2731.

Head-Smashed-In Buffalo Jump is one of the oldest, largest and best-preserved buffalo jumps in North America. For thousands of years, Plains Indians hunted buffalo by driving them over a cliff at the edge of the Porcupine Hills. The vivid name refers to the legend of a young Peigan man who watched the hunt from below the cliff and was found, with his skull crushed, under a pile of dead buffalo.

Today, Head-Smashed-In is a UNESCO World Heritage Site and one of the subtle wonders of Alberta. A $10-million interpretive centre, sensitively built to blend into the sandstone cliff, tells the story of the Plains Indians and their relationship with the buffalo. The surrounding grasslands and cliffs also harbour many secrets of this rich and ancient culture.

Although the centre was built and is operated by the Alberta government, the interpretive staff are local Peigan and Blood, fluent in English and Blackfoot and well versed in their ancestral legends and traditions. The story these descendants of the buffalo hunters tell on their group tours goes beyond conventional history into prehistory.

This was no primitive society. Hunting the massive, unpredictable buffalo without horses or guns required complex organizational skills involving hundreds of people. In years when buffalo grazed in the expansive basins above the cliffs, young men disguised under wolf and buffalo calf skins would lure and then push the herding animals into narrow drive lanes marked by stone cairns, some still evident. Farther along, hunters hidden behind brush piles would jump up, shouting and waving buffalo robes to keep the animals on course toward the cliff.

The hunters pressing from behind were aided by a visual deception that made the land above and below the cliff appear as an unbroken line of grassland. By the time the buffalo reached the precipice, they were ideally at full gallop, unable to stop or veer to the side to avoid the fatal plunge.

As visitors overlooking the cliff might guess, the 10-metre drop often didn't kill the animals outright. The presence in deposits at the cliff base of countless thousands of arrowheads confirms that hunters armed with spears and arrows finished off the many survivors. The carcasses were then dragged to the flats near the tipi campsites for butchering.

Some cuts were eaten fresh, while other meat was dried and mixed with fat and berries to produce long-lasting pemmican. Over the centuries, some 3 million kilograms of rocks were hauled more than a kilometre to the tipi campsites, where they were heated in fires and dumped into water-filled pits to boil the meat and render grease. Almost nothing was wasted. Bones were fashioned into tools, horns into containers and hooves into rattles. Hides became blankets and tipi covers, while skulls were painted and used in religious ceremonies and prehunt rituals.

It was, by and large, a good life that sustained itself for thousands of years. It ended in little more than a century. The arrival of the horse and gun around 1730 soon made buffalo jumps obsolete; Head-Smashed-In was last used in the early 1800s. And by 1880, the herds of prairie bison that had once roamed the Canadian prairies in the tens of millions were virtually wiped out.

As the Plains Indians kept no written records, the story of the prehistoric hunt has largely been pieced together by archaeologists delving through the rich bone beds. From late spring to early fall, visitors can watch and talk to archaeological teams digging through the centuries below the cliff in search of clues that will add meat to the bones of history. Scientists know, for example, the site was likely first used as a buffalo jump 5,700 years ago, well before the first Egyptian pyramid was built.

Many of the archaeological prizes—including skulls, stone projectile points, hide scrapers and a rare leather pouch—have been added to displays in the interpretive centre. The displays are a mixture of legend, artifacts and a bit of artifice. As visitors enter the front door, they are confronted by a man-made 12-metre cliff, with three stuffed buffalo poised at its edge above a reconstructed archaeological pit below. Nearby is a theatre, where a film recreating the hunt appears so lifelike some viewers believe live buffalo are being driven off the cliff.

Visitors enter the centre at the cliff base, ascending to the top, where they emerge above the cliff. After taking a short walk to a viewpoint overlooking the jump, they return to the building, which is toured from top to bottom via a series of terraces, each with a theme. The first level orients the visitor to the ecology of the prehistoric plains and introduces the native account of the origin of man. The second level surveys how early Plains Indians lived and the third describes the hunt, including its spiritual significance. The fourth level depicts how the arrival of Europeans dramatically altered this ancient culture, and the fifth shows how archaeology has been used to uncover the past.

Fort Macleod

ROUTE: From the Highway 22 overpass, drive 145 kilometres south on Highway 2 and 4 kilometres east on Highway 3 to Fort Macleod.
DRIVING DISTANCE: About 150 kilometres one way.
NOTE: The Fort Museum is open daily 9:00 a.m. to 5:00 p.m. (until 8:00 p.m. in July and August), except January and February. Admission charged. Phone (403) 553-4703.

The arrival of the North-West Mounted Police on the prairies in 1874 paved the way for the orderly settlement of southern Alberta. From their base in Fort Macleod, the redcoats quickly rousted the American whisky traders, helped native people make the transition to reserves and provided assistance to new settlers. This trip to southern Alberta's oldest community visits a reconstruction of the original fort and tours perhaps the finest restoration of historic downtown buildings in southern Alberta.

The highway between Calgary and Fort Macleod roughly follows the old Macleod Trail, used for centuries as a north-south route by natives and, later, white explorers and traders. The four-lane highway takes the straightest line possible. By contrast, the Macleod Trail took a more meandering route, following the lay of the land and the line of least resistance. The trail was perhaps a migratory route for prehistoric peoples arriving in North America. It was later used by the Algonquian and then the Blackfoot Nation. Among the first white travellers were traders in the 1860s who hauled supplies by wagon from Fort Benton in Montana to Fort Edmonton. Cattle herds from Montana were also driven this way in the early 1880s. First named Blackfoot Trail, the name was changed to Macleod Trail to reflect the mounted police who patrolled this route from Fort Macleod. The historic trail finally fell into disuse with the construction of a railway between Calgary and Fort Macleod in the early 1890s.

Fenced off by homesteaders at the turn of the century, the abandoned route has largely disappeared under a cover of grass. There are still places where traces of the deep ruts made by heavy wagons are visible. On some roads leading west of Highway 2, local groups have erected commemorative wagon wheels where the old trail passed.

While the Macleod Trail is long gone, its influence remains in the towns along the highway. When nineteenth-century wagons made their way north from Fort Benton, they covered 16 to 20 kilometres a day. They required similarly spaced stopping houses along the way, where horses could be changed and passengers and drivers could spend the night. The houses were often located at river crossings, such as the one on the Sheep River at Okotoks. Reinforced by the arrival of the railway, the stopping houses led to such towns as High River, Nanton and Claresholm.

Not all such places survived. In the 1870s, buffalo hunter Henry Kountz built a stopping house along Willow Creek (northwest of present-day Claresholm) called The Leavings, in reference to where the wagons and stages left the creek. The North-West Mounted Police established a detachment there in 1886. Bypassed by the railway, the site was abandoned in 1903.

Fort Macleod was founded in 1874 when Metis guide Jerry Potts led a troop of 150 North-West Mounted policemen to an island in the Oldman River. Here, following their long trek

The Fort Museum, a representation of the original Fort Macleod.

across the prairies, the men erected a fort named after their commander, Colonel James Macleod. Exposed to flooding, the fort was soon moved 3 kilometres west to higher ground on the site of the Fort Museum.

The Fort Museum is a representation of the original fort, complete with thick log walls and palisades. Displays in buildings around the fort's perimeter tell the story of the Mounties, the aboriginal peoples of southern Alberta, and early settlers.

Among the buildings are a sod-roofed storehouse and the restored office of local lawyer Frederick Haultain, who became premier of the North-West Territories prior to the formation of Alberta and Saskatchewan as provinces in 1905. For many visitors, the highlight of a museum visit is the musical ride performed four times daily in summer by a mounted patrol dressed in replica 1878 NWMP uniforms.

While in Fort Macleod, it's well worth taking a walking tour of the impressively restored buildings of the historic downtown (tour brochures are available at the town's visitor information centre). The tour covers nearly 30 buildings, including wood-frame structures built in the late 1890s and brick and sandstone buildings from the early 1900s. The highlight is the 1912 Empress Theatre, the oldest operating theatre in Alberta. Renovated at a cost of $500,000, the theatre features one original leather seat and decorative neon tulips installed on the pressed tin ceiling in 1938.

The town of Fort Macleod was incorporated in 1892. Stimulated by the development of a railway and coal mines in the nearby Crowsnest Pass, the town's population by 1910 had reached 2,500. In the boom before World War I, Fort Macleod was promoted as the Winnipeg of the West and had rivalries with Lethbridge and even Calgary. But its promise never materialized, and today Fort Macleod is only slightly larger than it was in 1910.

Pincher Creek

ROUTE: From its interchange at Highway 2 South, drive 17 kilometres west on Highway 22X and then 160 kilometres south on Highway 22. Head east on Highway 3 for 20 kilometres and then 3 kilometres south on Highway 6. Pincher Creek can also be reached by Highway 2 south to near Fort Macleod and then Highway 3 west.

DRIVING DISTANCE: About 200 kilometres one way.

NOTE: Pincher Creek Museum and Kootenai Brown Historical Park, located at the south end of James Avenue in Pincher Creek, is open 10:00 a.m. to 8:00 p.m. from May through September and by appointment the rest of the year. Admission charged. Phone (403) 627-3684.

Pincher Creek is the centre of one of the oldest ranching areas in southern Alberta. It is also in the midst of a spectacular landscape, where the plains and foothills rise dramatically into the mountains. The scenery alone is worth the drive from Calgary. This trip tours the countryside and stops at one of the most diversified small museums in Alberta.

After the drive down from Calgary, it's worth taking a short detour off Highway 3 to Lundbreck Falls, where you can stretch your legs and admire this impressive plunge in the Crowsnest River. Anglers from around the world come to the Crowsnest, a rare combination of a small, clear river with sizable trout in a spectacular setting. Unfortunately, a stretch of river has recently been drowned by a reservoir created by the nearby Oldman Dam. Provincial wildlife officials have attempted to rectify the fishery's loss by placing small rock berms in the river to form protected pools.

From Lundbreck Falls, proceed directly to Pincher Creek or take the scenic, roundabout route via Burmis and Beaver Mines. The latter is a hilly approach that crosses the Crowsnest and Castle rivers.

Pincher Creek is named for a pair of horse trimming pincers apparently found on the creek bank by a North-West Mounted Police patrol. Its population of nearly 4,000 makes this the largest community along the southern foothills and a rare town to have survived being bypassed by a rail line. Although a large gas reservoir helps feed the economy, Pincher Creek owes its continued existence to a strong ranching tradition that goes back to the late 1870s.

These high plains and rolling foothills provided ideal conditions for raising cattle. The often fierce chinook winds that blew through Crowsnest Pass kept the range clear of snow much of the winter. Cattle could also escape occasional cold snaps and blizzards in coulees and stands of trees.

The area's excellent grasslands convinced the North-West Mounted Police at nearby Fort Macleod to set up a farm here for feeding and raising the force's horses. From that base grew a vibrant community of settlers and ranchers, some of them retired Mounties. The largest early ranch near Pincher Creek was the Stewart Ranche, owned by a member of an Ontario lumber family and sold in 1888.

There are still some sizable ranches in the area, including one spread owned by investors from France. Pincher Creek's continued ranching strength is celebrated by an annual rodeo and cowboy poetry reading competition. Pincher Creek's ranchlands also support a growing number of tall, three-bladed wind turbines, used to generate "green" electricity for Calgary and other centres.

The Pincher Creek Museum and Kootenai Brown Historical Park contains an unusual and impressive collection of log buildings dating back to the early 1880s. Here is the transplanted log home (circa 1880) of the Irish-born Kootenai Brown. His remarkable resumé included the following careers: soldier, miner, buffalo and wolf hunter, whisky trader, guide and scout, gold prospector and dispatch rider. He was twice married to native women, once escaped the capture of Sitting Bull, and was acquitted of a U.S. murder charge. Yet he is best known as a prime mover in the creation of a national park at Waterton Lakes, where he lived for many years.

In 1885, another remarkable man, Oblate missionary Albert Lacombe, built in Pincher Creek a temporary church that is now located in the park. Father Lacombe was an important influence on the Blackfoot and Cree and lobbied tirelessly for native aid programs and government-sponsored Catholic schools.

Pincher Creek still has a strong French Catholic community, thanks to the efforts of Quebec missionaries who encouraged western settlement. The first German settlers in Alberta also came to the Pincher Creek area in 1883. In 1916, Doukhobors from British Columbia established a number of nearby colonies, where they hoped to quietly farm and pursue their pacifist religious beliefs. A Doukhobor barn and bathhouse from near Cowley have been relocated to the Kootenai Brown Historic Park.

On the return to Calgary, consider taking a back route

north on Secondary 785. Nearby, the flow of three rivers—the Oldman, Crowsnest and Castle—has been harnessed at the Oldman Dam and reservoir, one of the most controversial developments in Alberta's history. Nearby are the Three Rivers Rock and Fossil Museum—(403) 627-2206—and Heritage Acres Museum—(403) 627-2081. The latter features an unusual "village" of miniature buildings constructed from glass telephone insulators.

Continue north and east on this gravel road, which leads through some of the most spectacular rolling ranchlands in southern Alberta. The road eventually passes Head-Smashed-In Buffalo Jump en route to Highway 2.

Crowsnest Pass

ROUTE: From its interchange with Highway 2 south, drive 17 kilometres west on Highway 22X and 160 kilometres south on Highway 22. At the Highway 3 junction, turn right and drive 10 kilometres west to reach the Leitch Collieries and the beginning of the Crowsnest Pass tour.
DRIVING DISTANCE: About 200 kilometres one way.
NOTE: The Frank Slide Interpretive Centre is open daily 9:00 a.m. to 8:00 p.m. in summer and 10:00 a.m. to 5:00 p.m. the rest of the year. Phone (403) 562-7388. The Bellevue Underground Mine tours operate 10:00 a.m. to 6:00 p.m. from May until September. Phone (403) 564-4700. Admission charged for both.

The Crowsnest Pass is one of the finest destinations in Alberta. The windswept foothills provide a dramatic foreground to the sudden rise of the Rocky Mountains, which frame the long, low Crowsnest Pass. The pass is also rich in coal-mining history, tinged with the tragedies of the Frank Slide and the Hillcrest explosion, the worst mine disaster in Canadian history. Though the coal-mining era is over, its history is well preserved at excellent museums and interpretive stops.

A day trip hardly does the area justice. If time is limited,

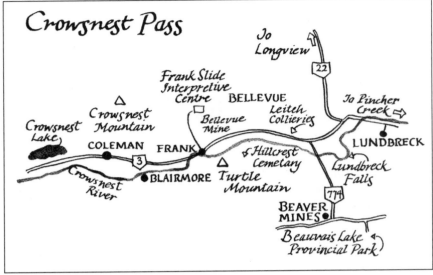

Crowsnest Pass

Jo
Longview

22

Frank Slide
Interpretive
Centre   BELLEVUE

Jo Pincher
Creek

Crowsnest
Mountain

Leitch
Collieries

Crowsnest
Lake

Bellevue
Mine

COLEMAN   FRANK

LUNDBRECK

3

Hillcrest
Cemetary

Lundbreck
Falls

Crowsnest
River

BLAIRMORE   Turtle
Mountain

774

BEAVER
MINES

Beauvais Lake
Provincial Park

head for the Frank Slide Interpretive Centre, which gives a good overview of Crowsnest Pass history. The alternative is to stay overnight. The pass is well stocked with motels and good campsites, the finest of which is at Beauvais Lake Provincial Park to the near south.

Located 40 kilometres north of the U.S. border, the Crowsnest Pass is the most southerly highway and railway corridor through Canada's Rocky Mountains. There are five communities strung along this 32-kilometre corridor to the B.C. border, which marks the Continental Divide. In 1979, these towns were amalgamated into the Municipality of Crowsnest Pass, population 6,600.

Archaeological surveys indicate extensive use of the pass by prehistoric cultures, dating back perhaps 10,000 years. One Kootenai Indian summer campsite discovered at Crowsnest Lake is 8,500 years old.

Among the early white visitors were members of the Palliser Expedition of 1857-1860 who explored the area extensively as part of their reconnaissance mission through Canada's western prairies. Large deposits of coal were noted by G.W. Dawson in an 1882 survey conducted for the Geological Survey of Canada. But the first industrial activity was the establishment of a sawmill around 1880.

The real impetus for development in the Crowsnest Pass was the arrival in 1898 of a Canadian Pacific Railway line, built to serve the lead, copper and zinc mines of southeast British Columbia. The deposits of soft bituminous coal were perfectly situated to fuel the railway's steam engines and to heat the homes of an influx of prairie settlers.

The boom was on, and soon the Crowsnest Pass developed into Alberta's largest coal-mining region. The five communities that exist today were formed between 1898 and 1905, as were numerous coal-mining ventures. Not all survived.

Leitch Collieries, located at the east end of Crowsnest Pass, was one such failure. Established in 1907 as one of the largest mines in the pass, it suffered from strikes and poor markets and went out of business in 1915. When the mine closed, the buildings from the nearby company town of Passburg were moved to surviving communities. Fortunately, the remains of the mine manager's house, power house, coal washery, tipple and a row of 101 coke ovens have survived. They are preserved as a provincial historic site at the Collieries, which can be toured on foot.

On the other side of the highway is the pretty community of Hillcrest, where a large cemetery graphically tells the town's sad history. In 1914, a huge explosion ripped through the tunnels of Hillcrest Mine, killing 189 men and boys and leaving more than 500 widows and children behind.

Such tragedies were not uncommon in the area's coal mines, where the high concentrations of methane gas and coal dust were a lethal mix. Between 1902 and 1912, more than 350 people died from explosions, helping the coal mines of Alberta and British Columbia earn the worst safety records in the world at the time.

The Crowsnest Pass's most famous tragedy was not an

Remains of the Leitch Collieries, a provincial historic site.

underground explosion, but the Frank Slide. In the early morning of April 29, 1903, more than 80 million tonnes of limestone slid off the face of Turtle Mountain, sweeping across part of the sleeping town of Frank and continuing well up the other side of the valley. An estimated 70 people were killed. Many scientists believe the slide was likely triggered by coal-mining tunnels in a mountainside already inherently unstable. Indeed, aboriginal peoples had long called Turtle "the mountain that moves." Perhaps not surprising in such a deadly industry, the mine reopened 30 days later, only to close for good in 1917.

Today, visitors flock to the Frank Slide site to marvel at the enormous jumble of boulders that litter the valley. While visiting the Frank Slide Interpretive Centre, it's well worth taking a 1.5-kilometre interpretive loop walk through the debris. Living among the boulders are pikas and golden-mantled ground squirrels, both usually found in rocky terrain at higher elevations.

While all the coal mines in the Crowsnest Pass are now

closed, visitors can don a miner's helmet and lamp and follow guides through part of the nearby Bellevue Underground Mine. The mine, originally owned by a company based in Lille, France, opened in 1903 and operated until 1962.

Another industry that prospered briefly in the Crowsnest Pass was rum-running. During Alberta's prohibition era from 1916 to 1923, liquor was smuggled across the border from British Columbia and sometimes Montana in fast cars and then bootlegged to thirsty patrons. One of the ringleaders was Emilio Picariello, known as Emperor Pick, who owned the Alberta Hotel, now a pharmacy in Blairmore. Cases of smuggled liquor were apparently taken from the hotel through a tunnel under the road and loaded onto railway cars. Picariello was hanged in 1923 after a policeman was killed in a shootout.

The westernmost community in the Crowsnest Pass is the sizable Coleman, where many old downtown buildings, such as a theatre and police barracks, are being restored to their coal-era grandeur. Visitors can also tour the Crowsnest Museum. Just beyond Coleman are outcroppings of 93-million-year-old volcanic rock, one of the few places providing surface evidence of volcanic activity in Alberta.

Sundial Medicine Wheel

ROUTE: From the Highway 22X overpass at Calgary's southern outskirts, drive south on Highway 2 for 83 kilometres. Just past Parkland, head east on Secondary 529 for 36 kilometres and then south on Highway 23 for 16 kilometres to Carmangay. Drive through the town to its northeast corner and then go 30 kilometres east on a good gravel road. Just before a big transmission line, turn south at a small Northstar Energy sign and drive 0.8 kilometres on a small road to a cattle guard. Proceed straight ahead up a rough, rocky track (watch your oil pan on passenger cars) to the fenced Sundial Butte.
DRIVING DISTANCE: About 165 kilometres one way.

NOTE: While accessible to the public, Sundial Medicine Wheel is an archaeological site protected by law under the Historical Resources Act of Alberta. Do not disturb it in any way.

Alberta is blessed with ancient rocks, from the magnificent upthrust of the Rocky Mountains to the deep sedimentary layers that trap rich pools of oil and natural gas. Southern Alberta also contains the majority of North America's medicine wheels—ceremonial circles of stone built and used by Plains Indians over thousands of years. This trip offers a rare opportunity to visit one of these sacred sites and a chance to tour some fine, overlooked country southeast of Calgary.

The tour begins by heading swiftly south down the twinned Highway 2 to Parkland, where a turn to the east suddenly sheds all traffic. The roughly paved Secondary 529 is initially straight as a rifle shot, bisecting flat prairie that occasionally dips into the Little Bow River Valley. A short detour south on Highway 23 passes the four-elevator village of Champion and soon thereafter the Carmangay tipi rings. Such circles of stone were used by native people to hold down the edges of their hide tipis; in some cases, they were expanded to form medicine wheels.

Just beyond is the quiet town of Carmangay, named for C.W. Carman and his wife, Gertrude Gay, who owned a turn-of-the-century wheat farm there. The town was moved to its current location in 1909 to meet the advancing rail line, necessitating the construction two years later of a wooden bridge. The bridge was replaced in 1928 by a striking steel structure that still stands.

This century-old history appears a blink of the eye compared to the trip's destination a little farther east. As if to advertise something momentous, the landscape soon changes from generally flat and expansive to abruptly undulating, the telltale sign of a stagnating glacier that left behind alternating troughs and hilly deposits. There are other clues that this was

The central rock pile, or cairn, of Sundial Medicine Wheel.

an excellent area for a medicine wheel—the prolific scattering of lichen-covered rocks among the short prairie grasses and the magnificent vantage point atop the highest of these hills, where sits Sundial Medicine Wheel.

Indeed, upon clambering to the top of the hill, your gaze is immediately drawn to the stupendous views across the fingered gullies of the deeply carved Little Bow Valley. Visible to the north is the upstream Travers Reservoir, which provides irrigation water to 73,000 hectares of surrounding prairie farms. But attention soon turns to the unique collection of rocks at one's feet.

Sundial Medicine Wheel comprises a bushy rock pile, or cairn, and two surrounding circles of rocks connected by a passageway. It fits into one of eight general forms of medicine wheels—some have lines of stones extending away in the four cardinal directions from a central circle—and is the only one of its type in Alberta with a double circle.

Like many of the 43 archaeological sites in Alberta containing medicine wheels, Sundial has not been scientifically excavated, and its date of construction is thus not known. But excavations 60 kilometres to the northeast reveal that the Majorville Medicine Wheel was first built perhaps 4,500 years ago and, except for a few interludes, continually used and added to thereafter. Southern Alberta's last medicine wheels were constructed by the Blood in the 1940s.

Medicine wheels were built and used for a variety of ceremonial and religious purposes, such as to mark a successful buffalo hunt or to commemorate a great battle or an important chief. In some cases, the chosen location apparently marked the residence, grave or death site of a warrior chief. While medicine wheels, and the meanings of the various forms, are not well understood, they remain important spiritual sites. At Sundial, for example, pieces of coloured cloth have recently been tied around several rocks.

Back on the main gravel road, it's worth driving a few kilometres farther east and descending into the Little Bow Valley, which is amazingly deep and wide considering the tiny river that now flows through it. A variety of routes can be taken on the return trip to Calgary, with the distant mountains of the Livingstone Range commanding the western skyline.

Calgary to Lethbridge

ROUTE: From its junction with Highway 2 south, drive 37 kilometres east on Highway 22X. Turn south on Highway 24, which farther south becomes Highway 23. At the junction with Highway 3, turn left for the final 17 kilometres to Lethbridge.
DRIVING DISTANCE: About 200 kilometres one way.

This approach to Lethbridge cuts through the heart of southern Alberta farming country and provides a more scenic alternative to the busier Highway 2.

About half an hour from the city limits, the route crosses the Bow River at the Carseland Dam. The dam supplies water through irrigation canals and storage reservoirs to farmers' fields around Lomond and Vauxhaull. First built in 1910, the dam was needed to raise the river levels sufficiently to divert water down a 67-kilometre canal to McGregor Lake.

An unfortunate side effect of such irrigation dams on the Bow is a decrease in spring flooding, which normally provides the wet mud needed for cottonwood seeds to germinate. Low flows through the summer may also cause these giants to die.

There are still stands of cottonwoods and balsam poplar growing in Carseland Provincial Park along the south banks of the placid Bow. The lush growth along the riverbanks provides a rich habitat for a diversity of birds. This is a good bird-watching area, especially during spring and fall migrations. One of the more interesting summer residents along this stretch of river is the white pelican. Other people are attracted by the large brown and rainbow trout that make this stretch of the Bow one of the prime angling rivers in the world.

The principal farm centre between Calgary and Lethbridge is Vulcan. The major crop in this area is winter wheat, planted in late summer and harvested the following August. Vulcan's 12 elevators have a storage capacity of more than 2 million bushels of grain, the largest volume of any primary grain-shipping point in Canada.

Long the dominant architectural feature on the prairies, the wooden elevator is fast disappearing in many small rural towns, the victim of abandoned rail lines. Many have been demolished and others sold for a dollar to be used as museums or even tea houses. In some places, the wooden structures are being replaced by huge concrete elevators, which are less dusty and more efficient, but certainly lacking in charm.

Farther south, it's worth stopping at the Carmangay Campground, on the banks of the Little Bow River. This scanty stream feeds the dammed Travers Reservoir downstream. The reservoir is a major cog in the Bow River Irrigation District, which waters more than 73,000 hectares of otherwise parched prairie. Some of the reservoir's irrigation water is also used to create a treed oasis at Little Bow Provincial Park, a short distance to the northeast.

Within a small grassy patch at the Carmangay Campground are nine tipi rings. These circles of stones were once used by aboriginal peoples to hold down the edges of their hide tipis. When the camp was moved, the stones were left behind. Archaeological discoveries of broken tools and buffalo bone fragments indicate the site was used sometime between A.D. 200 and A.D. 1700. These early inhabitants were probably attracted here not only by the buffalo but also by the availability of wood and water in a sheltered valley.

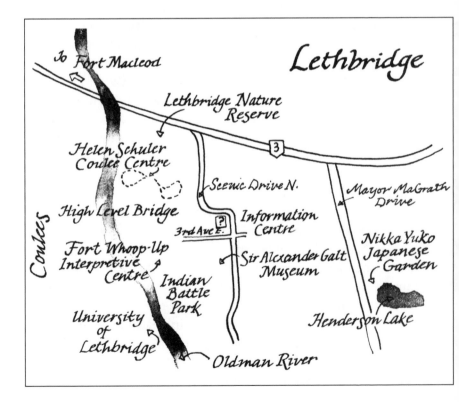

South of Carmangay is Nobleford. Here, in the depths of the 1930s Depression, prosperous farmer Charles Noble invented the Noble blade, a landmark in dryland farming. The blade broke the soil and killed weeds but left stubble and other surface debris intact, thus preventing erosion that was blowing many drought-era farms away. For many years, the Lethbridge-made Noble cultivator was sold throughout North America. A small heritage park at Nobleford displays a succession of these blades.

Lethbridge

Lethbridge is arguably the most varied and interesting mid-sized city in Alberta. It is blessed with both history and natural history.

The relative flatness of the southern prairie is relieved here by the deep Oldman River Valley. The valley harbours two distinct ecosystems—the cottonwood flood plains and the dry coulees—which can be toured on interpretive trails. Nearby, you can visit a reconstruction of the notorious whisky trading post called Fort Whoop-Up, see the origins of the city's coal mining, and overlook the site of the last Indian battle in Alberta. Indeed, it's easy to spend a whole day in the river valley alone.

The bluff overlooking the valley provides a view of two impressive pieces of architecture—the railway bridge that spans the Oldman Valley and, across the way, the ground-hugging University of Lethbridge, designed by Arthur Erickson. The bluff is also the site of the Sir Alexander Galt Museum, one of the finest small museums in Canada.

Lethbridge is Alberta's third-largest city with a population of more than 70,000. It is an important commercial centre for the irrigated farm communities of southern Alberta and is home to a number of light manufacturing and food processing plants.

Lethbridge is renowned for its strong winds and long hours of sunlight. It also gets my vote as the cleanest city in Canada. Where else can you find such immaculate parks, complete with receptacles containing bags for scooping dog poop? On an early Sunday morning in Henderson Lake Park, I discovered an attendant with a long broom dusting the eaves of a wooden bathroom. The adjacent Nikka Yuko Japanese Garden is even more carefully groomed.

Although it takes a couple of hours to get to Lethbridge, a visitor could devote several days to sampling its delights. The day tripper is advised to take small bites and digest them well, returning for more helpings at a later date.

Living and dying cottonwood trees on the Oldman River flood plain in Lethbridge.

Henderson Lake Park and Nikka Yuko Japanese Garden

ROUTE: From Highway 3 east in Lethbridge, take Mayor Magrath Drive south to North Parkside Drive, which provides access to the park and the Japanese Garden.
NOTE: The Nikka Yuko Japanese Garden is open daily from mid-May to early October. Admission charged. Phone (403) 328-3511.

Located just off a major commercial strip, Henderson Lake Park and the attached Nikka Yuko Japanese Garden provide a quiet respite from the bustle of this growing city. Indeed, the Japanese Garden is designed as a place of serenity and meditation.

Developed for the International Dry Farming Congress in 1912, Henderson Lake is the city's oldest major park. The 47-hectare park offers a diversity of recreational facilities, such as a lawn bowling green, a golf course, a swimming pool, tennis courts, boat rentals and a stadium.

Yet this can be a most tranquil spot in the early morning or evening for a peaceful amble on the expanse of lawn beneath tall trees or along the water's edge. The lawns, walkways and buildings are immaculately maintained. You wouldn't dare drop a candy wrapper here.

Immaculate is just the starting point for the 1.6-hectare Japanese Garden, an artistic interpretation of nature. It has been precisely designed and constructed, down to the selection and placement of each tree, shrub and rock. The garden layout encompasses designs developed over a thousand years in Japan and also incorporates influences of the Canadian prairie.

A meandering path connects five areas—a dry garden, a mountain and waterfall, a stream, ponds and islands, and a prairie garden—each providing a different viewpoint. All of these elements surround a pavilion, built of rare cypress wood by artisans in Japan and assembled here. The overall intent is to create a haven where visitors can quietly contemplate the beauty and order of nature and find inner peace.

Built as a symbol of Japanese-Canadian friendship, the garden was officially opened by Prince and Princess Takamatsu of Japan in 1967. The garden also recognizes the considerable contribution of the Japanese-Canadian community in this part of southern Alberta. The first Japanese settlers came to the area early in the twentieth century to work as farmers and miners. In 1942, following the bombing of Pearl Harbour, some 2600 Japanese-Canadians living on the British Columbia coast were relocated here and put to work in sugar beet fields.

Indian Battle Park

ROUTE: From Highway 3 in Lethbridge, head south on Scenic Drive and then west down a hill on 3 Avenue to Indian Battle Park.

Indian Battle Park is situated in the Oldman River Valley, cut here to a depth of nearly 100 metres below the level prairie. This sheltered spot in the heart of Lethbridge harbours coulees, slopes of native prairie grasses and flowers, and flood plains of cottonwood forest.

Indeed, nature has outlasted civilization in the river valley. Repeated spring flooding drove residents by 1960 to the prairie benchlands. Today, the continued erosion of coulees in Lethbridge is claiming urban backyards and threatening some houses.

The 102-hectare park also harbours history. The valley bottom is the site of the last great Indian battle in North America, the first white settlement in Lethbridge, the first coal mines in southern Alberta, and the highest/longest viaduct bridge in the world.

Nikka Yuko Japanese Garden.

The park is named for an 1870 battle between the Cree and Blackfoot that started in a coulee across the river and ended by the Coal Banks Interpretive Site. The victorious Blackfoot called the area *Asinaawa-iitomottaawa*, or "Where we slaughtered the Cree," in reference to the estimated 350 Cree killed in the battle, compared with some 60 Blackfoot. A year later, a peace treaty was signed between the two nations.

The following attractions—Fort Whoop-Up, the Lethbridge Nature Reserve and Helen Schuler Coulee Centre, and the Coal Banks Interpretive Site—are all within Indian Battle Park.

Fort Whoop-Up

NOTE: The fort is open 10:00 a.m. to 6:00 p.m. Monday to Saturday, and noon to 5:00 p.m. Sunday from mid-May to early September, with reduced winter hours. Admission charged. Phone (403) 329-0444.

Fort Whoop-Up is a replica of the original 1869 post established by American whisky traders at the junction of the Oldman and St. Mary rivers, a short way downstream from this site. The fort's displays and hands-on interpretive programs tell the story of this lucrative, sordid and short-lived chapter in southern Alberta's history.

No longer able to sell whisky on U.S. Indian reservations, the traders moved north of the 49th parallel in the late 1860s to sell their doctored brew. They found a ready market here as the Blackfoot were too weakened by white diseases to repel such intruders and the Hudson's Bay Company had largely abandoned its trading area in what was then the North-West Territories.

Originally known as Fort Hamilton, Fort Whoop-Up became the centre of a series of whisky trading posts in present-day southern Alberta. Here, traders sold "whisky" and rifles to the Indians, primarily in exchange for buffalo hides, used to make machinery belts in the burgeoning industrial factories of the eastern United States.

Typically, an 80-cent bottle of pure alcohol was substantially diluted and spiked with such ingredients as red ink, cough medicine, tobacco, gunpowder and lye soap. A cup of this vile concoction was often sold for a buffalo hide worth six dollars. Through such trade in the 1870s, some 25,000 buffalo hides and 5,000 pelts of kit fox, wolf, coyote, badger and antelope were shipped by oxen-pulled "bull trains" to Fort Benton, Montana.

This illegal trade prompted the formation of the North-West Mounted Police. Arriving at Fort Whoop-Up in 1874, the Mounties found the traders had already fled. While the whisky traders were easily put to rout, it was by no means an end to drinking in the area. By 1885, the rugged coal-mining town of Lethbridge boasted 19 saloons and three breweries.

Lethbridge Nature Reserve and Helen Schuler Coulee Centre

NOTE: The Coulee Centre is open 10:00 a.m. to 8:00 p.m. Sunday to Thursday, and 10:00 a.m. to 6:00 p.m. Friday and Saturday from June 1 until the beginning of September, with reduced hours the rest of the year. Phone (403) 320-3064.

This 82-hectare nature reserve was set aside in the early 1960s to protect the area's diverse river valley habitats. The centre was built in 1980 to interpret these habitats to visitors. A display room features interactive exhibits on seasonal themes.

After an introduction at the centre, the reserve is best explored via its three interpretive walks, which amply demonstrate the valley's contrasting landscapes. On dry coulee slopes, one can find such desert-like species as prickly pear cactus and prairie rattlesnake. On the nearby flood plain are lush forests of tall cottonwoods that attract white-tailed deer, great horned owls and a variety of songbirds.

Two of the trails, Nature Quest and Oxbow, are 1-kilometre loops that explore the flood plain along the Oldman River. The meandering river has carved this wide valley, its spring floods and deposits of sediment bringing renewed life to the valley bottom. The dominant trees in this riverine habitat are the magnificent stands of tall cottonwoods, in various states of health.

The several species of cottonwoods found along southern Alberta's river valleys play an important role on the otherwise dry prairie. Densities of breeding birds and deer are high in these forests, which offer shelter and food. Beneath the cottonwood canopy are often layers of shrubs, herbs and grasses that add to the biological diversity. Even a dead cottonwood provides birds with cavities for nesting sites and with burrowing insects for food.

The cottonwood's biggest enemy is upstream dams, such as the Oldman Dam, which restrict spring flooding and thus prevent seeds from germinating. Research by the University of

Lethbridge and Alberta Environment is examining the possibility of altering the operations of such irrigation dams to help preserve these forests.

On the other side of the centre is the Coulee Climb, an interpretive trail into a much different world. The word coulee comes from the French *couler*, meaning to flow. In the Lethbridge area, coulees are steep-sided ravines cut primarily by surface runoff that drains from the prairies down into the Oldman River Valley. The majority of southern Alberta's coulees are aligned 70 degrees east of north, suggesting they have also been initiated by the strong chinook winds that tend to blow in that direction.

There is a marked difference in vegetation on the north- and south-facing slopes of coulees. The south-facing slopes, exposed to sun and drying winds, support desert-like plants such as cacti and prairie grasses adapted to low moisture levels. By contrast, the sheltered north-facing slopes absorb moisture, allowing shrubs of the valley to proliferate.

Coal Banks Interpretive Site

Just inside the Lethbridge Nature Reserve is a small open-air kiosk near the entrance of a long-abandoned coal mine. The kiosk's few exhibits relate how coal mining put Lethbridge on the map and made it the first industrial town in western Canada.

The first miner was Civil War veteran Nicholas Sheran, who arrived in 1874 to operate a ferry and mine exposed seams of coal along the banks of the Oldman River. Sheran sold his coal to the whisky traders and later to the North-West Mounted Police and settlements in Fort Macleod and Fort Benton. His second mine was at Coal Banks, a translation of a Blackfoot word meaning "black rocks."

In 1882, a coal company formed by eastern businessman

Sir Alexander Galt and his son Elliott began operating drift mines here to feed the steam engines of the new Canadian Pacific Railway. An inclined railway was built to transport coal from the valley mines up to the railway on the prairie level.

The company then shipped the coal to the CPR main line at Medicine Hat, first by a river steamer and barge operation and then by a narrow gauge railway. This railway, under lease to the CPR, was later extended west through the Crowsnest Pass to the coal mines of southeastern British Columbia. To improve the crossing of the Oldman River at Lethbridge, the railway completed the High Level Bridge in 1909. At 1,624 metres long and 96 metres high, it is the largest bridge of its kind in the world and an aesthetic delight.

In the mid-1880s, the hamlet of Coalbanks sprang up at the entrance to these mines. Many families moved up to the flats in 1885, when the town of Lethbridge was laid out and named for a coal company president who never visited the town. Under the Galt empire, Lethbridge was virtually a company town in its early years.

The family legacy is commemorated in the Sir Alexander Galt Museum, at the top of the bluff. This splendid small museum tells the area's history and provides stunning vistas over the river valley and surrounding prairie.

While coal and the railways launched Lethbridge, it was irrigation agriculture that finally put the town on solid footing. Again it was Galt, at the urging of Mormon settlers at nearby Cardston, who initiated Alberta's first large-scale irrigation project at the turn of the century. Galt's sugar beet industry at Raymond and his model farm near Lethbridge proved irrigation agriculture could work in the dry south, prompting an influx of settlers until the outbreak of World War I.

Alberta Birds of Prey Centre

ROUTE: From its junction with Highway 2 south, drive east on Highway 22X for 37 kilometres and then 125 kilometres south on Highway 24, which soon becomes Highway 23. At Nobleford, head east on Secondary 519 for 34 kilometres and then 15 kilometres south on Secondary 845 to Coaldale.
DRIVING DISTANCE: About 210 kilometres one way.
NOTE: The Alberta Birds of Prey Centre is open daily from 10:00 a.m. to 5:00 p.m. from May 1 to September 30. Admission charged. Phone (403) 345-4262.

You wouldn't expect birds at the top of the food chain to need much hospital care. Yet a surprising number of hawks, eagles, falcons and owls run afoul of barbed wire fences, power lines, vehicles, illegal hunters and other man-made and natural hazards. The Alberta Birds of Prey Centre in Coaldale is Canada's largest such facility, specializing in the rehabilitation and release of injured birds of prey. A visit to the centre offers a rare opportunity to see these fiercely independent birds up close and to watch a raptor demonstrate its flying skills.

The approach is a lovely country drive down the twisting Highway 23 toward Lethbridge (see Calgary to Lethbridge trip, pages 64-67). At Nobleford, the route swings east past a corn maze and the town of Picture Butte—which bills itself as Canada's livestock feeding capital—and then crosses the placid Oldman River, set in a valley of beautifully sculpted coulees. Just beyond is Coaldale, a 6,000-person cattle and grain centre and home of the Alberta Birds of Prey Centre.

The centre is located along 28 hectares of wetland, dredged from the prairie, which attracts nesting ducks, geese and shorebirds and visiting ospreys and pelicans. Most of the centre's longer-term residents have, at least temporarily, lost that freedom of flight. Injured birds of prey are brought here to be repaired, rehabilitated and returned to the wild. Some birds, however, cannot safely be released, usually because they have lost their wildness or ability to fly. Many of these raptors can be seen along the centre's Hawk Walk, sitting on perches with one leg secured by a soft leather strap. Birds on display here include various hawks, a golden eagle, a great horned owl, a peregrine falcon and even a turkey vulture; the latter were once common when bison roamed the prairies but are now rarely seen in Alberta.

Large enclosures nearby house such species as the short-eared owl, ferruginous hawk and European eagle owl; the latter two are the world's largest species of hawk and owl, respectively. A recently constructed eagle centre allows recovering bald and golden eagles to stretch their wings in a 2,600-square-metre, wire-enclosed exercise aviary.

Some of the centre's recovering birds are turned loose for daily training and exercise. Trained hawks, falcons and owls are used in flying demonstrations (four times a day), in which a bird flies to the end of a field and then swoops back to the trainer's protected arm to receive its reward of a dead, day-old chick. Most raptors do not usually drink water, receiving their

The European eagle owl is the world's largest species of owl.

moisture from the flesh of their victims, which range in size from grasshoppers and mice to rabbits. Visitors can also slip on a leather gauntlet and have a live falcon or owl perch on their arm for a photo.

Despite the presence of some impressive aerial hunters, the Birds of Prey Centre's real star is a pocket-sized owl that nests underground, usually in ground squirrel burrows. The burrowing owl is an endangered species on Alberta's prairies, the victim of vehicle collisions, farm pesticide use and the loss of grasslands to crops. Operation Burrowing Owl is an attempt to reintroduce these strange-looking birds to their native habitat and to educate landowners about the importance of their conservation. The Birds of Prey Centre is playing its part by hosting a sizable captive breeding program that has released burrowing owl offspring into Canada's four western provinces.

Cardston/Remington-Alberta Carriage Centre

ROUTE: From the Highway 22X overpass, drive 210 kilometres south on Highway 2 to Cardston. The Carriage Centre is located on Main Street.
NOTE: The Remington-Alberta Carriage Centre is open daily 9:00 a.m. to 6:00 p.m. May 15 to mid-September, and 10:00 a.m. to 5:00 p.m. the rest of the year. Admission charged. Phone (403) 653-5139.

A day trip to Cardston might seem a long haul at two-plus hours of driving. But consider the drivers of oxen-propelled bull trains in the late nineteenth century, who would feel fortunate to cover 25 kilometres in a day. If you can't imagine those dark ages, a visit to the $12.4-million Remington-Alberta Carriage Centre will certainly acquaint you with the long-forgotten era of the horse-drawn carriage. While in Cardston, it's worth visiting the famed Mormon Temple and touring the restored, historic downtown.

Cardston is reached by driving south on Highway 2 from Fort Macleod. The high, open plains here provide expansive views of Alberta's southern Rocky Mountains to the west and some mini badlands to the east. The most impressive peak is Chief Mountain, just across the U.S. border. This massive chunk of rock, separated by erosion from the surrounding peaks, is a sacred mountain to the Blackfoot Indians. Young native males still ascend the peak in search of a spirit to guide their lives.

The highway soon drops and crosses, in quick succession, the Waterton and Belly rivers, which flow northeast to join the Oldman River. Their ample flood plains are cloaked in tall cottonwoods, poplars and shrubs, providing a rich habitat for wildlife on these otherwise treeless plains.

Just beyond the rivers, the road passes through the Blood Indian Reserve, the largest reserve in Canada. The 7,500-member band operates a sizable farm and ranch, launched at the turn of the twentieth century. Historically a nomadic, buffalo-hunting people reputed to be fierce warriors, the Bloods by the mid-nineteenth century were trading with the American Fur Company and the Hudson's Bay Company. In 1872, the Bloods burned down Conrad's Post, a new American whisky-trading fort. Soon after, they signed Treaty Number 7 with the Canadian government and in 1880 moved onto the reserve.

The clean, quiet town of Cardston is nestled in the foothills of southwestern Alberta, a short drive from Waterton National Park. A main-street program has led to the restoration of the façades of buildings dating to 1890. A central historical site is the little log house built by the founder of Cardston, Charles Ora Card, in 1887. That year, Card led 10 families from Utah by covered wagon to establish a Mormon colony here. Free from the religious persecution they felt south of the border, these immigrants settled in mud-chinked log houses and in the late 1890s helped develop the first major irrigation system in Alberta.

In 1923, they completed the Alberta Temple, the first such Mormon structure outside the continental United States. One of only two such temples in Canada, it now serves some 70,000 Latter-day Saints in western Canada and Montana. Recently restored, this massive, geometric structure maintains a commanding presence over Cardston from its hilltop perch. While the temple is open only to Mormons in good standing, the general public can tour a visitor centre at its entrance.

The major tourist draw to Cardston is the Remington-Alberta Carriage Centre, the vision of local rancher and businessman Don Remington. He collected and restored 49 carriages, creating the basis for the current collection of more than 200 horse-drawn vehicles, one of the largest such collections in North America. They range from the crude bull train wagons to elegant carriages that whisked the aristocracy to social functions. At this hands-on facility, you can sink into deep leather seats, learn how to handle buggy reins, discover the etiquette of riding in New York's Central Park, or even go for a real horse-drawn carriage ride along Lee Creek.

The Alberta Temple, in Cardston, one of two such Mormon temples in Canada.

Allow at least two hours to tour this facility, which covers the golden era of the horse-drawn carriage in detail. It's hard to believe now that such carriages were an all-purpose means of transportation. They were used to haul goods, build roads, shelter shepherds, deliver milk, fight fires, and transport passengers.

Fuelled by rapid industrial expansion in the late nineteenth century, the carriage trade boomed. Several thousand companies built carriages, the largest of them producing 100,000 vehicles per year in a variety of styles. Foreshadowing the development of the automobile, carriage makers introduced such concepts as mass production and showrooms, called repositories.

Those properly worried about car pollution today should consider that in late-nineteenth-century New York City, there were more than 175,000 horses, each producing some 9 litres of urine and 22 kilograms of excrement per day. Imagine wading across those infested streets in a petticoat.

The museum tells this and many other stories through imaginative displays and more audio-visual presentations than you can shake a riding crop at. After touring the exhibit hall, visitors can wander through a livery stable, help harness a fibreglass horse in the tack room and watch faded carriages restored to shining life by craftsmen in the restoration shop. The highlight for many will be taking an outdoor ride in a Yellowstone coach—once a popular tourist vehicle in U.S. national parks—drawn by two Clydesdale horses.

The introduction of the horseless carriage, at first considered a vulgar and passing fad, all but eliminated the horse-pulled variety by 1920. Some continued to be used until the 1950s, particularly on farms and in the delivery of milk and other goods. In recent years, the horse-drawn carriage has been regaining popularity as a recreational vehicle that harkens back to an era when life was pursued at a more leisurely pace.

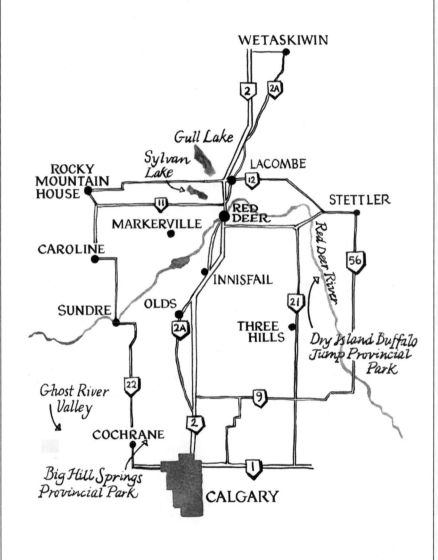

North

WETASKIWIN

2   2A

Gull Lake

Sylvan
Lake   LACOMBE

ROCKY   12
MOUNTAIN
HOUSE   STETTLER

11
MARKERVILLE   RED
DEER

CAROLINE   56

INNISFAIL

SUNDRE   OLDS   Red Deer River

2A   21
THREE
HILLS   Dry Island Buffalo
Jump Provincial
Park

Ghost River   22
Valley

9

2
COCHRANE

1
Big Hill Springs
Provincial Park   CALGARY

North of Calgary

For many Calgarians, any trips taken north of the city follow the straight and narrow four-lane Highway 2 to Edmonton. While the passing farmland is pleasant enough, this no-nonsense route misses some of the most appealing parts of Alberta.

Perhaps the most pleasant surprise for the adventurous day tripper is the countryside east of Highway 2 and north of Drumheller. Far from being dreary prairie, this is, instead, an enchanting land of often hummocky hills and intimate valleys. In summer and fall, the surrounding fields are vibrant shades of green and yellow.

So, too, are all the rich farmlands of central Alberta, which seem to be immeasurably enhanced when bisected by a narrow strip of undulating highway. The black soils that reach their productive peak in the Red Deer area yield bumper crops of barley, wheat, canola and hay, and sustain beef, cattle and hog operations. One trip in this section, to Olds College, provides a chance to learn more about the farm economy that puts food on our tables. Another journeys to the Markerville area, where immigrants from a diversity of countries arrived to farm.

Much of central Alberta is located in the aspen parkland region, a meeting place of the southern prairies and northern forests. This region also contains several fine recreational lakes, which the day tripper can sample at Sylvan Lake. Unfortunately, much of the native trees and prairie grasses in the parkland have been removed or ploughed under to take advantage of the fertile soils.

Some remnants of native landscapes, however, have been preserved and can be visited on these northern trips. They include the Rumsey Ecological Reserve, north of Drumheller, and the Red Deer River Valley, which in places like Dry Island Buffalo Jump Provincial Park provide spectacular examples of badlands terrain. Such sites also preserve the archaeological remains of First Nations camps, ranging from the prehistoric era to the 1800s, when this area was ruled by the Cree and Blackfoot.

Other northern trips into history can be taken by boarding an old-fashioned steam train in Stettler, viewing the restored antique cars at the Reynolds-Alberta Museum in Wetaskiwin or travelling through the forested foothills to Rocky Mountain House, site of several fur-trading posts. Not all northern trips are expeditions. Often overlooked on Calgary's doorstep is the charming Big Hill Springs Provincial Park, which is close enough for an impromptu stroll or picnic.

Big Hill Springs Provincial Park

ROUTE: From the intersection of Crowchild Trail and Nosehill Drive N.W., drive 10.5 kilometres west on Highway 1A. Head north on Secondary 766 (Lochend Road) for 11 kilometres and west on Secondary 567 for 3.2 kilometres. A 2.5-kilometre access road leads south to Big Hill Springs Provincial Park. The park is a day-use area, open 7:00 a.m. to 11:00 p.m.
DRIVING DISTANCE: About 27 kilometres one way.

Big Hill Springs Provincial Park is a prairie oasis just 20 minutes from the city limits. Jammed within its 26 hectares are spring-fed wetlands, cool forest, prairie grasslands and a rich human history. Much of this diversity can be experienced on a short interpretive hike. Pack a picnic lunch or supper, and

A profusion of cow parsnip in the understorey of an aspen forest.

you've got all the makings for a great escape from the city.

Be forewarned: Big Hill Springs is often crowded on warm spring and summer weekends. To quietly watch birds or hike in solitude, arrive early in the day. Take care also to preserve this tiny jewel. Stay on the main trails and do not pick the wildflowers or plants.

The park is located at the south end of Big Spring Coulee, where spring waters run down the hillside and into Big Hill Creek. The entire Big Hill Valley was carved during an early ice age by melting waters that emptied near Cochrane into the massive Glacial Lake Calgary. That lake is long gone, but beavers have built dams within the coulee along Big Hill Creek, creating a small lake and an extensive marsh.

The marsh, near the park entrance, and adjacent woodlands provide prime habitat for migratory and breeding birds. The diversity of birds seen here includes bald eagles, prairie falcons, northern saw-whet owls, rufous hummingbirds, great blue herons and two rarities—the sharp-tailed sparrow and the yellow rail.

Prehistoric aboriginal peoples were drawn to this area by the year-round supply of spring water and the shelter and wood provided by the valley forests. Discoveries of buffalo bones and ancient camps lead archaeologists to believe a nearby cliff was used as a buffalo jump.

At the turn of the century, nearby ranchers and even Calgarians would arrive at Big Hill Springs by horse and buggy for a leisurely day of picnicking. In 1891, D.M. Radcliff chose the coulee for Alberta's first commercial creamery, a water-powered operation later moved to Red Deer. Half a century later, the province built a trout hatchery along the spring. Its failure is commemorated by the remains of a concrete foundation.

The heart of Big Hill Springs Provincial Park is best seen by taking a looping 1.6-kilometre interpretive walk that starts behind a stone fireplace. The trail immediately enters cool forest and follows the course of the descending spring waters, which run in braided streams through grasses. The gray formations along the way are tufa mounds, deposited by spring waters of sufficiently warm temperatures and low pressures. An exposed tufa ridge nearby was formed by a once-dammed and now-abandoned stream channel.

In late spring and early summer, the aspen woods are filled with western Canada violet, shooting stars, wild roses and star-flowered Solomon's seal. The trail climbs to a viewpoint overlooking two narrow valleys carved by meltwaters from retreating glaciers and now adorned by prairie grasses and sandstone outcrops.

The proximity of the surrounding prairie is evident up here in the encroachment of crocuses, sage and fescue grasses. A small stand of willows, marking the transition from prairie to forest, soon gives way to the dappled light of thicker aspen forest, home to a variety of songbirds. From the high side of the valley, the trail descends steadily through spruce trees and a dense ground cover of cow parsnips, indicative of seeping water underground.

Ghost River Valley

ROUTE: From the Canada Olympic Park traffic lights, drive 18 kilometres west on the Trans-Canada Highway, 13 kilometres north on Highway 22 to Cochrane and 13 kilometres west on Highway 1A. Go north on Forestry Trunk Road 40 for 24 kilometres and turn west onto a gated rough gravel road (just past Richards Road). Follow it for 16 kilometres to a hilltop parking area.
DRIVING DISTANCE: About 85 kilometres one way.
NOTE: The hilltop overlooking the Ghost Valley can be reached in a car, but a high-clearance vehicle, preferably with four-wheel drive, is recommended for the steep hill and rocky riverbed crossings beyond. Otherwise, it's a 3.5-kilometre hike or mountain bike ride to the Black Rock trailhead (see below).

Here's an opportunity to put that sport utility vehicle to its intended use. The rough ride into and up the windswept Ghost River Valley is rewarded by panoramic views and steep walls of limestone that attract rock and ice climbers. It's also a chance for ambitious hikers to scramble to the abandoned fire lookout at the summit of Black Rock Mountain and gaze over the front ranges, forested foothills and prairies.

Despite its proximity to the city, the Ghost Valley is unknown to many Calgarians, though the black "thumb" of Devil's Head in its midst is a prominent peak west of the city. The lack of a four-lane access highway and glaciated majesty are more than offset by a sense of wildness and isolation that you won't find around Banff or Lake Louise.

But don't expect wilderness tranquility, either. This valley is a favourite destination for all-terrain vehicles, dirt bikes and random camping in large trucks. The Ghost and, especially, the parallel Waiparous Valley to the north are also infamous

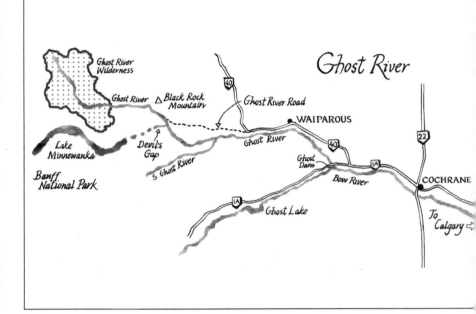

Ghost River

Ghost River
Wilderness

Ghost River △ Black Rock
Mountain

Ghost River Road

WAIPAROUS

Ghost River

Lake
Minnewanka

Devil's
Gap

S. Ghost River

Ghost
Dam

Bow River

COCHRANE

Banff
National Park

1A

Ghost Lake

To
Calgary

for their long weekend parties, though enforcement is being stepped up against these thoughtless offenders. Still, the Ghost Valley is often quiet, and considerable opportunities exist for rambles to places frequented by few people.

The approach to the Ghost Valley is a lovely drive in itself, particularly in the fall, when the yellow aspen make a lovely contrast with stands of dark green spruce and Douglas fir. From the 1A Highway turnoff, the paved forestry trunk road winds north through a wide valley of grassy foothills and gradually thicker forest, passing by the tiny communities of Benchlands and Waiparous along the way. Once onto the bouncy Ghost River Road, it's worth stopping at 4 and 6 kilometres for splendid views up the valley to peaks of the Palliser Range such as Mount Aylmer, straddling the Banff National Park boundary.

The next viewpoint is the 16-kilometre hilltop parking area. Straight ahead are the steep yellow limestone walls of

Phantom Crag, one of many rock- and ice-climbing cliffs in the Ghost. To the right, the gravelly main channel of the muted Ghost River can be followed upstream by off-road vehicle past Black Rock towards Devil's Head and then on foot all the way to its headwaters below Aylmer Pass, some 30 kilometres distant.

To the left, another valley leads through Devil's Gap to Lake Minnewanka; high-clearance vehicles can be driven for a couple of rough kilometres to the Banff park boundary. This route was used by early natives to reach the mountains and was later followed by nineteenth-century explorers, including Sir George Simpson, head of the Hudson's Bay Company, and later James Hector of the Palliser Expedition. It was also the scene of battles between the plains Blackfoot and the mountain Kootenay, and Indian graves apparently line the riverbanks. According to native legend, ghosts wandered the riverbank, picking up the skulls of those killed in battle, hence the name Ghost, though Palliser called it Dead Man River.

The modern-day river is a ghost of its former self, thanks to

Hikers descending towards the Ghost River Valley from Black Rock Mountain.

a 1942 diversion canal that channels much of its water through Devil's Gap into the dammed Lake Minnewanka in Banff National Park. (If you walk or drive through Devil's Gap, the diversion channel is mainly hidden behind a rock ridge.) Water from the Ghost thus helps generate power at both the Cascade station (beside the Trans-Canada Highway east of Banff townsite) and at Ghost Lake, where the river merges with the Bow River west of Cochrane along Highway 1A. Immediately downstream of the diversion canal, the Ghost River channel is dry most of the year, except when water is released into it during high stream flow. Farther downstream, groundwater and surface runoff cause the river to resume its flow.

While the Ghost Valley has been significantly impacted by water diversions and by humans seeking recreational diversion, some 15,000 hectares of its upper watershed have long been protected within the Ghost River Wilderness. This area, which swings north along the Banff boundary to the Ghost River's source, can be explored on foot by backpackers prepared for some route finding, bushwhacking and perhaps encounters with grizzly bears. Much of the lower Ghost Valley, other than the valley floor, is also being included in the new Don Getty Wildland Park and thus should be better protected from future impacts.

Black Rock Hiking Option
This 5-kilometre hike climbs 900 vertical metres to an abandoned fire lookout on a good trail that gets steeper and somewhat exposed near the rocky summit of Black Rock Mountain. Good boots are needed, especially for the initial descent of somewhat slippery rock from the summit. To reach the trailhead from the hilltop parking area (about 3.5 kilometres by vehicle, bike or foot), descend the steep hill, turn right on a gravel track that swings left to cross the rocky riverbed and then turn right again (cairn) on a smaller side road. The trail

starts in woods on the far side of another riverbed crossing.

The well-beaten trail soon bends left and begins climbing through stands of lodgepole pine and spruce to open slopes that provide glimpses east over the foothills. Above treeline, the trail swings left onto a ridge, then back right through a gap in limestone cliffs to an open bench. A final push up the summit block's switchbacks leads to the windowless old lookout, now clad in cedar shake siding. This 2,460-metre, windswept perch offers tremendous views west to Devil's Head and the upper Ghost Valley, north to the Waiparous Valley and east across the prairies. On a clear day, you can see Calgary's downtown office towers.

The Black Rock Mountain Lookout was built in the late 1920s and early 1930s, with the building's timber and later supplies hauled up by pack horse. A telephone line was erected to provide communications with the nearest ranger station. Constructed on four cement blocks and heated only by a one-burner gas stove, the building was often cold and drafty; one attendant said he mostly stayed in his sleeping bag during bad weather. The lookout was closed in the early 1950s and replaced by the Mockingbird Lookout to the northeast.

Wool Tour

ROUTE: From the Airport/Delacour Road overpass, drive 6.4 kilometres north on Highway 2, 22 kilometres east on Secondary 566, and 26 kilometres north on Highway 9. From Beiseker, continue north on Secondary 806 to Linden and then 15 kilometres west to reach Custom Woolen Mills. From the mill, drive south on a gravel road to Secondary 581, which is followed west across Highway 2 to Carstairs. Follow the signs west and south to PaSu Farm.
DRIVING DISTANCE: About 140 kilometres one way.
NOTE: Custom Woolen Mills is open Monday to Friday 9:00 a.m. to 5:00 p.m. Phone 337-2221. PaSu Farm is open 10:00 a.m. to 5:00 p.m. Tuesday through Saturday, and noon to 5:00 p.m. Sunday. Phone 337-2800 or 1-800-679-7999.

Petting sheep at PaSu Farm.

Alberta is cattle country. The pre-eminence of the barons of beef is obvious to anyone touring the ranchlands or passing the feedlots of southern and central Alberta. Yet there is a small but growing sheep industry in the province. More people are eating tender, farm-raised lamb and buying woollen garments with a "Made-in-Alberta" stamp.

This outing tours through the farmland of south-central Alberta en route to two unique sheep-based establishments. The first destination is Custom Woolen Mills, where raw wool is processed into various products using machinery normally found in a museum. The second stop is west at PaSu Farm, a working sheep farm with the added comfort of a retail gallery and a high-ceiling dining room.

Early on, the odds were stacked against sheep on the prairies. In 1881, much of the arable land in southwest Alberta was carved into 100,000-acre (40,470-hectare) ranching leases and stocked with grazing cattle. One of these giant spreads, at Cochrane, briefly replaced cows with 8,000 sheep, herded north from Montana. A spring snowstorm, a prairie fire and low prices spelled the end of the sheep operation within three years. Farther east, an even larger sheep herd was brought north by entrepreneurial Englishman Sir John Lister-Kaye. But this, too, failed.

These experiments were the exception. While this area was spared the range wars waged between U.S. cattle ranchers and sheep farmers, federal legislation restricted sheep grazing leases in western Canada until 1903.

The route to Custom Woolen Mills is a pleasant drive through farmland northeast of Calgary. The urban sprawl is quickly replaced by rural solitude on narrow highways bordered by fields of grain, sloughs and roadside grasses.

Highway 9 passes through Irricana, settled in the early 1900s when both Canadian Pacific and Canadian Northern built railways through the village. The name comes from the irrigation canals that flowed through this productive farmland. Just outside Irricana is Pioneer Acres, home of a ploughmen's and threshermen's club and an impressive collection of vintage farm machinery. The second weekend in August, the club hosts a show and reunion that one year attracted 8,000 people.

Just beyond Irricana is Beiseker, where a restored 1910 CPR station is now home to a museum, library and village office. Farther north, the road drops into a valley near the junction of Kneehill and Lonepine creeks, which eventually empty into the Red Deer River near Drumheller. Nearby is the village of Linden. It has overcome the lack of a railway and grain elevators by building an agriculture-based manufacturing industry that includes a feed mill.

Situated on farmland to the west is Custom Woolen Mills, the only complete wool-processing plant still operating in western Canada. This is a virtual working museum because its wool is produced on carding machines, spinning mules and other machinery dating back to 1868. The small plant, owned by Fenn Roessingh and husband Bill Purves-Smith, is open during operating hours to curious visitors who can watch the smoothly clicking and whirring antiquities at work.

All the mill's products are made from virgin wool sheared off western Canadian sheep. Because these sheep live in a cold climate, their wool has more loft and is often of better quality than imported wools. The raw wool is turned into natural-fibre comforters, mattress pads, sleeping bags and socks, as well as carded wools and yarns for knitting. These and other products are sold in a small gift shop and by mail order to customers across Canada.

From Custom Woolen Mills, it's a half-hour's drive west on gravel highways to reach PaSu Farm. Along the way, the road passes through Carstairs, established as a ranching community and now also serving dairy-farming and grain-growing industries.

PaSu, named for owners Pat and Sue deRosemond, is a working ranch that features some 12 breeds of sheep, many of which spend their summers grazing in hills to the west. The meat is sold to retail markets and the wool processed at Custom Woolen Mills to produce such things as wool blankets. These and other products—including moccasins, fine wool fashions, sheepskin coats and hides—are sold in an extensive gift shop.

Attached to the shop is an airy restaurant, offering visitors a light lunch, Sunday buffet or suppers and specializing in European cuisine and lamb dishes. This building opens onto a yard, where visitors can pet the sheep and admire the view of distant mountains. Those staying overnight can book a room in a recently completed bed and breakfast.

PaSu welcomes scheduled tours, where visitors learn how wool is washed, dyed, carded and spun. These must be booked in advance. PaSu also hosts the annual Canadian Classic Sheepdog Trials.

Olds College

ROUTE: From the Airport/Delacour Road overpass, drive 74 kilometres north on Highway 2. Take the Olds exit and drive 5 kilometres west on Highway 27. Olds College is on the eastern outskirts of town, along the 2A Highway.
DRIVING DISTANCE: About 80 kilometres one way.
NOTE: The Olds College campus is open 8:15 a.m. to 4:30 p.m., Monday to Friday. Individuals are free to tour the campus facilities but may wish to join a Friday afternoon tour. Phone (403) 556-8281 or toll-free 1-800-661-6537.

At the turn of the century, some 80 per cent of Albertans were directly or indirectly employed in the farm economy. Today, only 3 per cent of the population works on the farm. Many city slickers have never visited a farm and experienced walking through a mucky barnyard, riding a tractor, baling hay or milking a cow. Thus, it's not surprising if they think bacon comes from the grocery store and barley from a beer bottle.

Now there's a chance to fill in those rural gaps by going to agricultural school for a day. This does not involve enrolling in a course on growing crops or running a feedlot. Rather, it's a self-guided tour of Olds College, one of the top agricultural institutions in Canada. In a couple of hours, visitors can view horses, beef cattle, hogs, sheep and horticultural displays. You can also talk to barn managers about new farming methods and, if you're lucky, help milk a cow.

Since it opened as the Olds School of Agriculture and Home Economics in 1913, the college has provided education and training in a variety of agricultural fields. Olds graduates become farm managers, agronomists, nursery operators, golf course greenskeepers, blacksmiths, veterinary assistants and grain inspectors, to name a few occupations.

The college is also a leader in agricultural research. Its scientists, students and industry partners conduct experiments on such things as developing improved grasses for athletic fields, recycling swine and dairy waste and investigating goat genetics.

The 600-hectare campus features a natural arboretum and buildings that range from modern glass structures to those built by early settlers. The Olds College Farm, which opened in 1911, is the largest teaching and demonstration farm in western Canada. It contains cereal, hay and pasture land, and houses nearly 3,000 animals in its horse, beef, swine, sheep and dairy barns.

Following a stroll through the campus, visitors should head to the barns, where a variety of species are raised and bred, often using the latest techniques in artificial insemination. In the dairy facility, for example, such technology has produced Holstein cows that produce 32 kilograms of milk a day. On one visit, I got a chance to attach an automatic milking device to the cow's teats. The udder felt like a warm silk purse.

Another interesting stop is at the sheep facility, where a variety of breeds can be petted over the fence. At the equine enterprise, horses are bred, trained and showed. You might also check the swine building for fresh litters of piglets.

While in Olds, it's worth touring the town's historic downtown. Many of the buildings, dating back to the turn of the century, feature tall oak and brass doors (a tour brochure is available at the town's tourist information office). The area's first settler was David Shannon, who arrived in 1890 in an open hand-rail car and applied for squatter's rights. Olds has overcome devastating fires in 1922 and 1978 to become a prosperous agriculture and energy-based town.

For a more scenic return to Calgary, drive south on the two-lane Highway 2A, once the main highway between Calgary and Edmonton. In summer, the roadside fields of canola are a brilliant yellow. The highway passes near the farming community of Didsbury, first settled by Mennonites from Waterloo County, Ontario. The freeway is rejoined north of Airdrie.

RCMP Dog Training Centre and Innisfail

ROUTE: From the Airport/Delacour Road overpass, drive 92 kilometres north on Highway 2 to the RCMP Dog Training Centre (along the highway). To reach Innisfail, drive another 7 kilometres north on Highway 2 and exit west on Highway 54.

DRIVING DISTANCE: About 100 kilometres one way.

NOTE: Free tours of the dog training school (about 1.5 hours long) are offered every Wednesday at 1:30 p.m. from late May until the end of September. Phone (403) 227-3346 or e-mail: policedogs@rcmp-grc.gc.ca.

If it's true that the Mounties always get their man or woman, it's often their dogs that do the legwork leading to the arrest. This tour of the only Royal Canadian Mounted Police (RCMP) dog-training centre in Canada is a fun family outing that consists of viewing a short video, touring kennels and watching the young German shepherds (and their trainers) go through an obstacle course and chase down a "suspect." The day can be rounded out in nearby Innisfail by visiting historical sites, taking a nature walk and perhaps enjoying a cup of tea.

The RCMP began formally training its police dogs in 1937 and has based its canine training facilities near Innisfail since 1965. At any time, about 6 teams of dogs and their handlers—RCMP officers from across Canada—are at this rigorous, 5-month boot camp. During 80 training days, the dogs learn to track, search, attack and hold, and detect bombs and drugs. To graduate, they must be able to perform these tasks while, say, on slippery floors, in heavy crowds or under gunfire—at all times remaining under the firm control of their handler.

As their run through the obstacle course shows, the dogs must fearlessly jump over barriers, climb through open windows and scramble up and down steep stairs. The tour's highlight comes when one dog chases a trainer playing a villain,

A German shepherd collars a "suspect" during a demonstration at the RCMP Dog Training Centre.

seizes a padded arm and detains the suspect until released by its handler. While the dogs are trained to hold—not savagely attack—a culprit, their bites can be considerable; several handlers have needed stitches when a dog's teeth found a thin spot in the padding during these exercises.

The RCMP uses only German shepherds (usually young males) because of their versatility, strength, courage and ability to work in cold climates. A number of young trainees have been imported from the Czech Republic, where German shepherds are used as border guard dogs and have not been bred for show. The Innisfail training centre has started raising its own puppies, not only to hasten the learning curve but also to forego the $6,000 to $8,000 cost of buying a dog. The price of a good trained dog, particularly those capable of detecting bombs, has soared since the September 11 terrorist attacks in the United States.

Just north of the dog training centre, in the heart of Alberta's most productive farmland, is the town of Innisfail. In 1754, fur-trade explorer Anthony Henday passed near here in a vain attempt to convince the Blackfoot people to trade with the Hudson's Bay Company. His trip, however, helped convince his employers to establish a string of fur-trading posts along major rivers west of Hudson's Bay. He also was apparently the first white man to see the Rocky Mountains.

The area's more recent history is celebrated at the Innisfail Historical Village, which features restored buildings, artifacts and pioneer farm machinery. One highlight is The Spruces, an 1880s stopping house that once stood seven kilometres north on the old Edmonton-Calgary Trail, on the site of a winter supply cache used by the Palliser Expedition in the late 1850s. The historical village is open from late May to Labour Day, Tuesdays to Sundays, and serves afternoon tea on Fridays at 2 p.m.

High tea, as well as lunch, can also be enjoyed at the nearby Dr. George House, open May to September. Built in 1893, it housed the first museum in what was then the Northwest Territories; Mrs. George later designed Alberta's original provincial crest. This historical house still harbours a small museum and has a memorial rose garden on its grounds. On the western outskirts of Innisfail is the Napolean Lake Natural Area, which contains a 1.4-kilometre self-guided nature trail through an aspen parkland forest filled with late spring and summer flowers.

Calgary to Red Deer

ROUTE: From the Airport/Delacour Road overpass, drive 130 kilometres north on Highway 2. The Red Deer Information Centre is at Heritage Ranch, accessed from the highway, at 134 kilometres.

Judging by the steady stream of traffic at any time of day between Calgary and Edmonton, one would think this route through Red Deer had a long and glorious past. But it wasn't until the relatively recent date of 1875 that wagon wheels carved the Calgary-Edmonton Trail onto the land. Until then, natives and later explorers and missionaries had taken various other routes north to reach the Fort Edmonton area. The establishment of Fort Calgary by the North-West Mounted Police in 1875 created a need for a more direct line. This was accomplished by opening a fork of Reverend John McDougall's trail between Fort Edmonton and his mission at Morley, to the west of Calgary. The fork branched south from near present-day Bowden to Fort Calgary.

In the early days, the wagon track extended south to Fort Benton, Montana, where eastern goods were unloaded from steamboats on the Missouri River. The goods were then transported north on bull trains—a string of heavy wagons pulled by teams of oxen. North of Calgary, however, the bull trains bogged down in the soft black soils.

To solve this problem, the bull trains were replaced on this stretch by Red River carts. These all-wood carts with ungreased axles produced a horrible, squealing sound. But they were lightweight and manoeuvrable, easy to repair on the trail and could be floated across rivers. The principal river crossing on the Calgary-Edmonton trail was the Red Deer River near today's Red Deer.

The arrival of the railway in Calgary in 1883 brought settlers to the west and greatly increased traffic on the Calgary-Edmonton Trail. Within a few years, passengers could ride between the two towns on open stagecoaches for the princely sum of $25. A five-day trip in good weather, it often took much longer when rain, snow or fog moved in. In winter, the snow often disappeared south of Olds, forcing the coaches to switch from runners to wheels.

To serve these passengers, stopping houses were strategically placed along the route. Between Calgary and Red Deer, they included Dickson's (near today's Airdrie), Scarlett's (northeast of Carstairs), Lone Pine (near Bowden), Content's (near Innisfail) and Miller's (near Penhold). The accommodations at these early "motels" ranged from the luxury of a bed with cotton sheets to sleeping on the floor.

The trail quickly fell into disuse upon the completion in 1891 of the Calgary and Edmonton Railway, which roughly followed the trail's route. The railway, however, did lead to the creation of towns at sidings and stations along the way. The stations were spaced about every 30 kilometres, with the sidings halfway between. Between Calgary and Red Deer, these towns are Airdrie, Crossfield, Carstairs, Didsbury, Olds, Bowden, Innisfail and Penhold. Many were named for towns in England and Scotland or after employees of the Canadian Pacific Railway.

The trail was back in business in 1906 when G. Corriveau and his son made the first recorded automobile trip from Edmonton to Calgary, covering the distance in less than 12 hours. After 1910, car traffic increased steadily and the dirt trail was upgraded to gravel and finally to pavement.

Much of the original highway followed the present-day 2A Highway. It was replaced in the 1950s by today's Highway 2, a high-speed road that bypassed the towns created by the railway. Ironically, much of the four-lane, divided freeway between Calgary and Red Deer closely follows the original wagon route.

As you approach Red Deer, notice the bountiful crops in roadside fields. The black soils in central Alberta are the most fertile in the province, producing grains that have won championship awards as early as the 1893 World's Fair in Chicago. In the Red Deer area, the farms are one-third smaller than the provincial average, with no loss in production.

Nearly half the cultivated land here is devoted to barley, primarily used for feeding livestock and producing malt in beer. Another major use of farmland is to produce the hay and forage crops used to feed more than 100,000 beef cattle in the area. There are also a number of dairy farms, where black-and-white Holsteins produce milk.

Red Deer

Like many Calgarians, I used to consider Red Deer a strip of highway gas stations halfway to Edmonton. No longer. Red Deer, I've discovered, is a great place for nature and history buffs.

The city has one of the best urban river park systems in Alberta and an excellent nature centre. Even if you only have

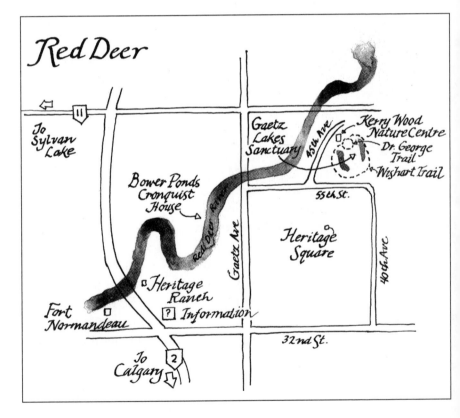

an hour or two, you can take a walk in the woods or embark on a quick family bike ride along the Red Deer River. The park system can be quickly accessed from the Visitor Information Centre at Heritage Ranch, alongside Highway 2.

Across the highway is the historic Fort Normandeau, site of the first Red Deer settlement and home to a reconstructed North-West Mounted Police post. Visitors can also explore Red Deer's past by touring a downtown square of heritage buildings or going on their choice of five historic walking tours.

Not all the interesting architecture is ancient. The semi-circular St. Mary's Church, for example, was designed and built by Douglas Cardinal in 1968 and inspired by a spider's web. At Red Deer College, the innovative Arts Theatre was designed by Arthur Erickson.

The name Red Deer is actually a misnomer. Scottish settlers mistook the area's elk for the red deer of their homeland. Thus, they called the river and the first village Red Deer, and the name stuck. The more perceptive Cree used the name *Waskasoo Seepee*, which means Elk River. Today, the city's river valley park system is called Waskasoo, helping alleviate a historical error.

Red Deer is Alberta's fourth-largest city, with a population approaching 70,000. It is the largest commercial centre between Calgary and Edmonton and an important supplier to the oil and gas industry. Yet Red Deer is perhaps best known for being in the heart of the province's most productive farmland.

Fort Normandeau

ROUTE: From the 32 Street interchange on Highway 2 in Red Deer, follow the Fort Normandeau signs west and north for 5 kilometres.
NOTE: Fort Normandeau is open daily, noon to 8:00 p.m., in summer. Phone (403) 347-7550.

Gaetz Lake Sanctuary in the heart of Red Deer.

Fort Normandeau, a reconstruction of an old military post, is located on the banks of the Red Deer River near a natural crossing of the river. The shallow water, slow current and low banks made this the best place to ford the river for 80 kilometres in either direction.

Used for perhaps thousands of years by natives, the crossing was also favoured in the late nineteenth century by Metis buffalo hunters and by commercial wagon-drawn freighters travelling between Edmonton and Calgary. To serve this traffic, McClellan's Hotel and a ferry began operating in 1884. A small community also sprang up at the crossing, where settlers could graze cattle and horses.

During the North-West Rebellion of 1885, Louis Riel and others led an armed rebellion of Metis and Indians upset about federal indifference to their grievances over land and self-government. While the few battles of the North-West Rebellion occurred to the east, settlers at the Red Deer River crossing were evacuated. Led by Lieutenant J.E. Bedard Normandeau, a group of soldiers fortified McClellan's two-storey stopping house to protect the settlement and keep lines of communication open.

The fort never saw action during the rebellion. For several years, it was used as a North-West Mounted Police detachment before being dismantled and rebuilt as a nearby farmhouse in 1899. The present replica of the fort was built in 1974, using some of the original logs. An interpretive centre now tells the story of the fort and the river crossing.

The crossing fell into disuse with the arrival of the Calgary and Edmonton Railway in 1891. Reverend Leonard Gaetz, who earlier owned a store at the crossing, offered the railway an interest in his land to the east in exchange for routing the line through his property, which soared in value. Thus, the town of Red Deer was located several kilometres downstream.

Across the river from the fort is the site of a federal industrial school for Indian children. They were compelled to leave the reserve and board at the school, where they were taught skills such as farming, carpentry and domestic work. This sorry chapter in native relations ended at the conclusion of World War I, when the school was converted to a training farm for returning soldiers.

Waskasoo Park

ROUTE: The park can be reached from Heritage Ranch, which houses a visitor information centre, on the east side of Highway 2, just north of the 32 Street overpass. To access other parts of the park, ask for directions and maps at the information centre.

NOTE: The information centre is open throughout the year. Phone toll-free 1-800-215-8946. Kerry Wood Nature Centre is open year-round. Phone (403) 346-2010. Web site: http://www.visitor.red-deer.ab.ca.

Red Deer is blessed with an excellent parkway system that snakes through the city along the Red Deer River. Named Waskasoo, the park boasts more than 50 kilometres of paved trails on which to cycle, walk and gain access to riverside picnic areas, recreational facilities and trout ponds.

The park can be quickly sampled by taking a short walk or cycle through a riverside forest below Heritage Ranch. Another favourite spot is Bower Ponds, overlooked by Cronquist House, a 1911 Victorian farmhouse fully restored as a municipal historic resource. If time permits only one destination, I recommend the excellent Kerry Wood Nature Centre and the adjoining Gaetz Lakes Sanctuary, where some 160 species of birds and mammals have been spotted.

The river valley through Red Deer is much different than farther downstream, where the bedrock has been severely eroded into wondrous badland formations. Here, a historically moister climate produced more vegetation, which provided a protective cover against intense erosion. Over thousands of years, the decay of this vegetation has created the black soils for which central Alberta is famous.

The rich soils around Red Deer have been both a blessing and a naturalist's curse. They produce Alberta's most bountiful crops and sustain a large livestock industry. But good farming has meant most of the native prairie and woodlands have disappeared under the plough. The remnant tracts of native vegetation are mainly found on steep slopes and in river valley bottoms, such as along the Red Deer River.

Fortunately, significant sections of these natural areas have been preserved in Waskasoo Park, a 1,000-hectare green space in the river valley. A walk along the shady river terraces below Heritage Ranch, for example, reveals aspen habitat that gives way in places to a succession forest of white spruce. In the latter, the accumulating litter of spruce needles has turned the soil acidic, allowing only selective plants like twinflowers and feather mosses to thrive.

The Red Deer River that placidly flows through the city originates in the Drummond Glacier area north of Lake Louise. As it tumbles out of the mountains and foothills, the river angles north toward Red Deer. A short distance before the city, it is slowed by the fairly recent Dickson Dam, which, by restricting spring flooding, has adversely affected downstream cottonwood trees.

Yet this is not the first time the river has been dammed. At the end of the last ice age, glacial meltwaters from the mountains were backed up by the stagnating continental ice sheet, creating the immense Glacial Lake Red Deer. Eventually the lake overflowed the ice dam, cutting a new route southeast and abandoning a previous channel to the east, now followed by the Battle River.

Visitors can learn more about the Red Deer River and other area habitats through the exhibits and interpretive programs at the Kerry Wood Nature Centre. The centre, named after a local naturalist, also has a good natural history gift shop.

The nature centre is at the entrance to the Gaetz Lakes Sanctuary, a federal migratory bird sanctuary since 1924. The sanctuary protects 118 hectares of spruce, poplar and mixed wood forest along with meadows, marshes and two oxbow lakes. The last are bow-shaped lakes formed in an abandoned channel of the river.

The shorter of two walks within the sanctuary is the Dr. George Trail, a 1-kilometre paved loop through poplar forest. A branch of the trail leads to a bird blind and viewing deck, where visitors can spot a diversity of waterfowl and songbirds through a telescope. The Wishart Trail is a more strenuous 4-kilometre walk that circles the West and East lakes, passing through meadows and deciduous and spruce forests and climbing to several lookouts.

Markerville-Dickson

ROUTE: From the Airport/Delacour Road overpass, drive 118 kilometres north on Highway 2. Take Highway 42/592 west through Penhold for 19.5 kilometres to its junction with Secondary 781. Continue west on a gravel road for 6.5 kilometres to Markerville. Stephansson House Provincial Historic Site is 9 kilometres to the north. From Markerville, drive 6 kilometres south on gravel Range Road 22, 8 kilometres west on Highway 54 to Spruce View, and 3.2 kilometres south to Dickson.

DRIVING DISTANCE: About 175 kilometres one way.

NOTE: Stephansson House is open daily 10:00 a.m. to 6:00 p.m. from May 15 to Labour Day. Phone (403) 728-3929. During the same season, Markerville Creamery (403-728-3006) and Dickson Store Museum (403-728-3355) are open 10:00 a.m. to 5:30 p.m. except for Sunday, when the latter opens at 12:30 p.m. Admission charged.

Pioneer home of Icelandic poet Stephan Stephansson.

The lovingly restored buildings of Markerville and Dickson provide a fascinating trip back to the pioneer days of central Alberta. A century ago, settlers from the distant countries of Iceland and Denmark cleared and drained homestead land to create farms and unique communities. The highlight of the trip is a tour of the restored house of Stephan Stephansson, a pioneer farmer by day and one of the Western world's great poets by kerosene light at night.

En route to Markerville, Highway 592 west passes through the rich farmland of central Alberta that usually produces bumper crops. The flat lands near Penhold were created by Glacial Lake Red Deer, a huge buildup of glacial meltwater at the end of the last ice age. Just north of Penhold is the Red Deer Industrial Airport, site of the renowned annual Red Deer International Air Show, featuring a dazzling display of formation and acrobatic flying. Phone (403) 340-2333.

Farther west is the Pine Hill Colony, one of a number of prosperous Hutterite communities in central Alberta. Like many settlers, the Hutterites came to Canada to escape religious persecution. They live communally in village-like settlements on large farms, where they grow cereal crops and vegetables, the latter often sold along with chickens at farmers' markets. Once a colony reaches a population of about 125, a spin-off group forms a new colony.

Located on the banks of the placid Medicine River, Markerville is a unique community in its origins and preservation of its pioneering past. The area was first settled in 1888 by a group of Icelanders escaping the droughts of the U.S. Dakotas. They were captivated by the lush, isolated parkland here, where they could maintain their customs and language.

The early struggles of homestead farming were greatly relieved by the creation in 1899 of a federal government-sponsored creamery, which became the community's economic lifeblood. Not surprisingly, the town's name was changed from Tindistoll to Markerville in honour of C.P.

Marker, dairy commissioner for what was then the North-West Territories. Under the stewardship of Daniel Morkeberg and later his son Carl, the creamery operated until 1972, producing some of Alberta's finest butter from area farmers' cream.

Now a provincial historic resource, the Markerville Creamery has been restored to its 1932 condition, complete with all the butter-making equipment of the period. Tours are conducted during the summer months and a small restaurant, the Kaffistofa, offers Icelandic dishes typical of a century ago.

The now quiet hamlet of Markerville has a number of other historical buildings, including a 1903 community hall, a 1907 Lutheran Church and a general store. For several decades, Markerville maintained its rich Icelandic culture, expressed in traditional dishes and woollen clothing, an Icelandic library and even a men's debating society.

As you take the short drive north to Stephansson House, consider the mix of nationalities that settled this area. The Icelanders were followed in 1903 by Danes, who homesteaded near Dickson, and later by Swedes, who farmed near Sylvan Lake. The area west of Markerville became known as Yankee Flats for the numerous American settlers. Despite this diversity, English language schools, new roads and increased communication with the outside world eroded the distinctiveness of these communities. By the 1930s, this area was much like any rural Alberta community. Today, perhaps 10 per cent of the Markerville area is of Icelandic descent.

Stephan Stephansson (1853-1927) arrived in the Markerville area in 1889. He was a community leader and hard-working pioneer farmer. But he was best known for his prolific, stirring and often controversial poetry, all written in Icelandic and after the day's work was done. Although little known in Canada, he is considered Iceland's greatest poet since the thirteenth century. Many Icelanders today make the pilgrimage to Markerville to visit Stephansson's house.

Visitors to this historic site are greeted by a costumed guide, who provides tours of the restored house and serves Icelandic cookies fresh from the oven. Stephansson built the house himself, originally a log structure that was expanded and refurbished to accommodate his family of eight children. He even constructed the desk where at night he wrote his poetry.

To the south of Markerville is Dickson, the oldest Danish settlement in western Canada. It was first settled in 1903 by seventeen Danes, who had earlier emigrated to the United States. Though inexperienced as farmers, they drained the boggy land around Dickson and helped establish dairy farming in central Alberta.

In 1991, the Dickson Store Museum was opened by Queen Margrethe II of Denmark. The store, beautifully restored to appear as it did during the 1930s, is stocked with groceries, hardware and dry goods typical of the period. Just to the south, the Danish Canadian Museum and Gardens has recently opened.

Sylvan Lake

ROUTE: From the Airport/Delacour Road overpass, at Calgary's northern outskirts, drive 137 kilometres north on Highway 2 to just past the Red Deer gas strip. Go 16 kilometres west on Highway 11 and then 3 kilometres north to reach the beach in the heart of Sylvan Lake.
DRIVING DISTANCE: About 155 kilometres one way.

For those who don't mind a crowded tourist setting, Sylvan Lake is a pleasant place to spend a day at the beach. It is one of the few lakes within two hours of Calgary that offer a sandy beach and reasonably warm and clean water to swim or play in. One can also canoe, wind surf, water slide, water ski, jet ski, fish or just take a long walk along the waterfront. It's the perfect place for active young families and teenagers.

Best of all, the town's beach is within Sylvan Lake Provincial Park, established in 1932. The park is essentially a 1.6-kilometre stretch of sandy waterfront backed by a thin strip of grass dotted with picnic tables. There is a sizable roped-off swimming area to protect paddlers from being terrorized by motorized boats. The park, which is wheelchair accessible, also contains picnic shelters, wash and change rooms and a playground.

On sunny summer weekends, it can be hard to find a parking spot, let alone a private space to build sand castles. But at other times, the pace is less frenzied and you can turn your back to the lakefront shops and gaze placidly across this sizable lake to the distant horizon.

Sylvan Lake has been attracting recreational visitors to its shores since the turn of the twentieth century. Early visitors were often nearby farm families, a number of whom were immigrant homesteaders from Scandinavia. In 1912, a Red Deer auto club made the first recorded motorized excursion to Sylvan Lake. To remove one broken-down car from the road, the women passengers pulled and the men pushed.

Better highways brought more tourists from central Alberta and beyond. Today, Sylvan Lake is one of the busiest lake resort towns in Alberta. It offers visitors the amenities of motels, campgrounds, shops, restaurants and a huge water slide. Besides the cottages that ring the lake, an increasing number of people, including Red Deer commuters, are living in the town year-round.

Another provincial park, Jarvis Bay, is 3 kilometres north of the town of Sylvan Lake on Highway 20. Though principally a campground, the park has several short trails through aspen and balsam poplar forest and down to the lakeshore. These can be accessed from a parking lot near the park entrance. Ask at the entrance booth for a park newspaper, which contains an area map showing the trails.

A more pristine spot is the Sylvan Lake Natural Area, an 11-hectare site that protects forested and shoreline habitats on the northwest edge of the lake. It is the only public land on the lakeshore still in a natural state. This moist transition zone between parkland and boreal forest harbours a variety of marsh plants, ferns and at least 30 species of breeding birds.

Unfortunately, trails and signs are minimal and it can be very wet underfoot. At such times, only the most persistent nature lovers and birders will enjoy the experience. To reach the natural area from the eastern edge of Sylvan Lake town, drive 9.7 kilometres north on Highway 20, 11.6 kilometres west on Rainy Creek Road, and 1.5 kilometres south on a narrow gravel road to a dead end. The scenic drive en route offers several magnificent views of forested hills and farmland.

For more prolonged views of this rolling topography, return to Calgary via Secondary 781, which heads south from the town of Sylvan Lake. The road passes through some of Alberta's finest farmland, where the black soils produce bumper crops of barley, wheat, hay and canola.

At a T-junction, head east on Highway 54 to regain Highway 2 south at Innisfail. Innisfail was once called Poplar Grove because of the area's abundant aspen forests. In the 1880s, it was a popular overnight stopping place for wagons carrying freight and passengers between Edmonton and Calgary.

Lacombe/Gull Lake

ROUTE: To reach Lacombe, either drive 153 kilometres north of the Airport/Delacour Road overpass on Highway 2 and then 3 kilometres east on Highway 12, or head 140 kilometres north on Highway 2 and then, just past Red Deer, go 23 kilometres east and then north on Highway 2A. Gull Lake is 16 kilometres west of Lacombe on Highway 12.

DRIVING DISTANCE: About 175 kilometres one way.

NOTE: Michener House Museum is open 10:00 a.m. to 4:00 p.m. daily from May to September. Admission by donation. Brochures ($1) for the self-guided tour of historical downtown Lacombe can be purchased there. Phone (403) 782-3933. This number can also be used to book tours of the Blacksmith Shop Museum. The Ellis Bird Farm is open 11:00 a.m. to 5:00 p.m. Tuesday to Sunday from late May to early September. Phone (403) 346-2211. Doug's Exotic Zoo is open daily from 10 a.m. to 7 p.m. from early May to the end of August. Admission charged. Phone (403) 784-3400.

Alberta has had an unfortunate tendency of bulldozing its all-too-brief history. So it's well worth taking a 90-minute drive north to Lacombe to see a rare prairie town that has preserved and restored many of its early twentieth-century buildings and maintained one of Alberta's finest Edwardian streetscapes. The Lacombe area offers day trippers other diversions, such as visiting a bird farm or an exotic zoo or strolling along the sandy shores of nearby Gull Lake in Alberta's oldest provincial park.

Those in a hurry can zip up Highway 2 and then go briefly east on Highway 12. This route enters Lacombe by its long and wide main street (50th Avenue), lined with stately two- and three-storey houses with high-pitched roofs. Fiftieth Avenue also crosses the old Calgary and Edmonton Trail, which in the 1880s was a pathway for wagons and Red River carts. A slightly slower approach to Lacombe is via Highway 2A, north of Red Deer, which crosses the placid Blindman River and winds through rich farmlands interspersed with industrial yards, llama and elk ranches and U-pick berry farms.

Lacombe is named after Father Albert Lacombe, an Oblate missionary who helped forge peace between first the Blackfoot and Cree in the mid-1800s and later between these nations and white settlers. Some of those settlers flocked here in 1881 with the arrival of the railway connecting Edmonton and Calgary. By the turn of the century, Lacombe was bigger

The Michener House Museum in Lacombe was the birthplace of former governor general Roland Michener.

than Red Deer and soon had a federal agricultural research station that developed the world-renowned Lacombe hog. Still in operation, the station is now noted for its meat-packing research. While Red Deer quickly eclipsed Lacombe as a major centre, the latter retains its small-town charm with a population of 9,000 people.

On the outskirts of downtown is Lacombe's oldest building, the Michener House Museum. Built in 1894, this Queen Anne-style house was originally the manse for the Lacombe Grace Methodist Church. In 1900, it became the birthplace of former Canadian governor general Roland Michener; his father, Edward, was the church minister. Restored by the local Maski-Pitoon Historical Society, the house was declared a provincial resource and in 1984 became a museum, housing community archives and Michener family artifacts.

A few blocks away is the Blacksmith Shop Museum, built in 1902 and one of only two Alberta blacksmith shops on their original sites. Today, the restored historic structure is a working museum where blacksmiths use turn-of-the-century tools and forging techniques to mould hot metal on anvils.

In the late 1980s, Lacombe became one of the first participants in Alberta's Main Street Program, using government monies to help restore its historic downtown buildings. Highlights include a brick-and-sandstone 1910 flatiron block, a building with a pressed tin ceiling and an old billiard hall that once hosted upstairs dances and gambling parties. A turn-of-the-century Chinese restaurant and laundry offered all-you-could-eat meals for 25 cents; the owner's wife became one of Alberta's first Chinese women after his partner helped pay a $500-per-head tax to bring her and their children to Canada.

Three kilometres north of Lacombe is Canadian University College, a Christian educational institution dating back to 1909 and run by the Seventh-Day Adventist Church. A church on the college grounds has a membership of 1,100 and thus boasts one of Canada's largest Adventist congregations.

Sixteen kilometres southeast of town is the Ellis Bird Farm, where nest boxes and birdhouses support healthy populations of mountain bluebirds, tree swallows, purple martins, flickers and black-capped chickadees. Visitors can stroll around the farm on a boardwalk trail, view a wetland habitat and enjoy lunch in a tea room. Twenty-six kilometres east of Lacombe, lions, tigers, jaguars, monkeys and zebras are among the more than 300 species on display at Doug's Exotic Zoo. Activities include pony and camel rides, children's amusement rides and miniature golf.

A good way to end the day is to drive west of Lacombe to Gull Lake and Aspen Beach Provincial Park, established in 1932 as Alberta's first provincial park. The park's waterfront offers a wide public beach and relatively warm waters for swimming. A boat launch provides access to the lake's deeper waters, where anglers can troll or cast for northern pike, yellow perch, walleye and lake whitefish. Beyond the beach's west end, an interpretive trail crosses a bird-rich marsh on an elevated boardwalk. Fifty years ago, this marsh was covered in water, but soon thereafter the lake's level mysteriously dropped, leaving some cottage owners stranded far from the waterfront. To ensure more predictable water levels, Alberta Environment has since periodically pumped water from the Blindman River into Gull Lake.

Rocky Mountain House National Historic Site

ROUTE: From the intersection of Crowchild Trail and Nose Hill Drive N.W., drive 23 kilometres on Highway 1A to Cochrane. Head north for 150 kilometres on Highway 22, which, en route, takes short jogs west near Sundre and Caroline. The final 7 kilometres to Rocky Mountain House is west on Highway 11. Rocky Mountain House National Historic Site is 7 kilometres west of town via Highway 11A.

DRIVING DISTANCE: About 190 kilometres one way.

NOTE: Rocky Mountain House National Historic Site is open 10:00 a.m. to 5:00 p.m., May to September. Phone (403) 845-2412.

Rocky Mountain House National Historic Site is the scene of a fascinating chapter in the fur-trading history of western Canada. Beginning in 1799, a series of forts operated here as a base for trading with Plains Indians and exploring farther west. Despite limited success in either endeavour, the forts persisted until 1875.

Today, the area is preserved as Alberta's only national historic site. Visitors can tour a small interpretive centre and take short walks along the North Saskatchewan River past the sites of four forts, fur-trading artifacts and a buffalo paddock. Interpretive displays and programs are offered throughout the park during the peak season.

Site of the original 1799 fur-trading forts at Rocky Mountain House National Historic Site.

The route from Calgary to Rocky Mountain House follows the edge of the lower foothills into the boreal forest of west-central Alberta. North of Cochrane, there are impressive views of the mountains, which soon angle away to the northwest. The rolling terrain is dotted with farms and ranches cut from a cover of aspen that progressively gives way to spruce. North of the Red Deer River, the boggy lowlands support extensive stands of American larch, which have deciduous needles that turn to a stunning gold in the fall.

Not surprisingly, logging is an economic staple in this heavily forested region. So, too, is oil and gas, particularly the removal of large quantities of sour gas, so-called because of its high concentrations of poisonous hydrogen sulphide. North of Sundre is the $1-billion Caroline gas plant, completed in 1992 to exploit a deep field containing some 2 trillion cubic feet of sour gas.

The sparkling foothills rivers also attract whitewater boaters and anglers. The nearby town of Caroline is famous for two things—the wary brown trout in nearby streams and multiple world figure-skating champion Kurt Browning.

Rocky Mountain House is the economic hub of this region with a population of more than 5,000. It also serves as central Alberta's gateway to the mountains. The scenic David Thompson Highway, which intersects the Icefields Parkway north of Lake Louise, is well worth taking as an alternative return to Calgary if time permits.

The major attraction here is Rocky Mountain House National Historic Site, located along the north shore of the North Saskatchewan River. The 228-hectare site protects the remains of four historic forts, a burial ground, archaeological sites and the surrounding natural landscape of forest, meadows and riverfront. The small visitor centre tells the area's fur-trading history through exhibits of aboriginal artifacts, archaeological discoveries and a replica trading room.

Much more can be learned by taking two interpretive walks. The longer 3.2-kilometre loop takes visitors to the sites of the first two forts, built in 1799 by fur-trading rivals, the North West Company and the Hudson's Bay Company. The two merged under the latter's name in 1821 and continued operating its fort here until 1835. The original intention of trading with the Kootenai Indians on the west side of the Rocky Mountains never materialized. Instead, Rocky Mountain House served the rival northern plains peoples, principally the Blackfoot Nation, which consisted of the Peigan, Blood and Blackfoot tribes. But other than a brief period during the 1820s, the trade for beaver pelts and, later, buffalo hides never prospered.

The North West Company fort also provided a base for the explorations through the mountains of David Thompson, arguably the greatest mapmaker in western Canadian history. Thompson's plans to forge a route from Rocky Mountain House through Howse Pass to the west coast were thwarted in 1810 by the Peigan, who wanted to prevent trade with the Kootenai. Thompson was forced to develop a more northerly route through Athabasca Pass near Jasper.

Near the 1799 fort sites are replicas of the large York boats, used by the Hudson's Bay Company to transport goods, and the birchbark canoes of the North West Company. Each year, voyageurs would make the round trip on the rivers between Rocky Mountain House and Lake Superior.

The food staple for these gruelling trips can be found in the nearby buffalo paddock. The Norwesters learned from native people how to dry buffalo meat into pemmican, a highly concentrated source of protein that saved the voyageurs from having to hunt for fresh meat during their paddling expeditions.

The shorter, 900-metre trail loops past the sites of the 1835-1861 and the 1864-1875 forts. The former was abandoned and then burned to the ground by a band of Blackfoot. Two chimneys from the latter are the only visible structural remains of the fur-trading era here.

The last fort closed in 1875, when the Hudson's Bay Company was convinced it was safe to build a post on the plains south of Rocky Mountain House. By then, the North-West Mounted Police had arrived and the once feared Blackfoot had been decimated by smallpox and the disappearance of the buffalo.

Dry Island Buffalo Jump Provincial Park

ROUTE: From the intersection of 16 Avenue and 68 Street N.E., drive 50 kilometres east on the Trans-Canada Highway. Turn left on Highway 21 and drive 102 kilometres north, to just past Huxley, and then 19 kilometres east on a good gravel road to Dry Island Buffalo Jump Provincial Park.

DRIVING DISTANCE: About 170 kilometres one way.

NOTE: Dry Island Buffalo Jump Provincial Park is a day-use area, open 7:00 a.m. to 11:00 p.m. from May through September. The park may be closed during wet periods when the steep entrance road becomes impassable. Phone (403) 442-4211 for current conditions.

Arriving at the bluff overlooking Dry Island Buffalo Jump is one of the most dramatic moments a motorist can experience in Alberta. Suddenly the grassy plateau drops away to reveal fantastically eroded badlands and their primary sculptor, the placidly winding Red Deer River. While any such perch over the Red Deer River Valley inspires awe, this is one of the most magnificent. Certainly, this approach provides the steepest descent through the geological ages to the valley bottom.

Dry Island Buffalo Jump Provincial Park (now there's a mouthful) has no campgrounds or trails. The idea is to marvel at the scenery without contributing to its rapid erosion. It's worth packing a picnic lunch, which can be consumed at tables near the Red Deer River. The rest of the day can be profitably spent visiting the nearby towns of Trochu and Three Hills.

The drive north on Highway 21 is one of the loveliest in central Alberta. Along the way, the road dips through several green valleys of considerable size. One might wonder how they were formed, considering the creeks—including Kneehills, Threehills and Ghostpine—that flow through them are scarcely noticeable. At the end of the last ice age, melting glacial waters and mountain runoff formed the huge Glacial Lake Drumheller behind the retreating continental ice sheet. The fingers of this lake reached up into the drainages you are crossing. When they drained, broad valleys were left behind.

From the viewpoint overlooking Dry Island Buffalo Jump Provincial Park, the Red Deer River Valley drops through 200 metres of badland terrain. It was created over the past 13,000 post-glacial years as the forces of water, wind and frost cut through the soft layers of exposed bedrock, which were laid down as marine sediments between 63 million and 68 million years ago.

In front of you is a large flat hill, or mesa, severed from the surrounding prairie by the eroding power of side streams. Because it was never surrounded by water, it is called Dry

Island. The prairie grasses atop the island have also never been disturbed by grazing, cultivation or, hopefully, television truck commercials.

The Buffalo Jump portion of the park name refers to a large cliff to the south, used several times by early native hunters to drive buffalo to their death. Tools, bits of pottery, fire pits and other evidence of processing camps unearthed near the base of the cliff indicate the jump was used at least four times between 700 and 2,800 years ago. This 45-metre buffalo jump is unusually high compared to others, such as Head-Smashed-In, near Fort Macleod, which in its prime had a mere 10-metre drop.

Dry Island was one of the more northerly buffalo jumps. Farther north, increased tree cover and different topography favoured other means of hunting, such as stalking and herding the animals into corrals. The later introduction of the horse and gun allowed native peoples to chase buffalo more directly.

Archaeologists were not the first whites to scour this landscape for buried treasures. Famed American palaeontologist Charles Sternberg rafted down the river here in search of fossils during the Great Canadian Dinosaur Rush, which reached its peak just before World War I. More recently, the bones and teeth of tyrannosaurus and dromaeosaurus were discovered here, along with the fossilized remains of clams, fish, turtles and birds dating back some 65 million years.

One can find refuge from the heat trapped in these arid badlands by descending steeply to picnic sites along the Red Deer River. Here, the moist valley floor supports the growth of cottonwood and aspen trees and an understorey of saskatoons and wild roses. This greenery provides shelter and food for a variety of birds and animals. Early morning and evening is a good time to see deer and coyotes along the river's edge.

A walk down to the river reveals slow-moving water that cuts into the soft banks and carries deposits of muds, silts and sands downstream. Across the river, tall stands of white spruce thrive in the cool, moist conditions of the steep and sheltered slope.

On the return trip south on Highway 21, it's worth stopping in Trochu, an exceptionally tidy prairie town that features a museum and an arboretum with some 200 varieties of trees and shrubs. On the outskirts of town is the St. Ann Ranch Country Inn, a provincial historic site that now boasts a tea house, bed and breakfast, and museum (1-888-442-3924). The ranch was formed in 1905 by a group of aristocratic cavalrymen from the Brittany area of France. While many left to defend their homeland during World War I, a few returned, including Ernest Frere. His grandson's family now owns the ranch.

A short drive south of Trochu is Three Hills, a strong Christian community with nine churches and the Prairie Bible Institute. It is one of the largest bible schools in North America, preparing missionaries for work around the world. Guided tours of the institute's campus and its 4,500-seat auditorium can be arranged by phoning (403)443-5511.

Rumsey Ecological Reserve

ROUTE: From the Airport/Delacour Road overpass at Calgary's northern outskirts, drive 125 kilometres to Drumheller via Highway 2 north and Highway 72/9 east. From Drumheller, drive 56 kilometres north on Highway 56 and turn east on Secondary 589, the Byemoor/Endiang Road. Follow it for 1.6 kilometres to the Rumsey Ecological Reserve, marked by small green signs on the south side of the road. Park at one of five small pull-offs over a 5-kilometre stretch.

DRIVING DISTANCE: About 185 kilometres one way.

NOTE: Though the ecological reserve is on Crown land, it is part of a grazing lease. It is considered a courtesy to ask the leaseholder's permission to walk on these lands. Contact ranch manager George Spencer at (403) 876-2370. Close all gates behind you and don't block them with your vehicle.

Covering 180 square kilometres, the Rumsey block is one of the largest uninterrupted tracts of native aspen parkland left in the world. To stand in the midst of this rolling terrain may be the closest thing to recapturing what central Alberta was like before the white man arrived.

In 1990, about 34 square kilometres of this block were set aside as the Rumsey Ecological Reserve. It has thus been protected from the fate of more than 80 per cent of Canada's aspen parkland, lost to farming and other development.

En route, it's worth stopping at Morrin (20 kilometres north of Drumheller) to visit a sod house built to honour the area's early pioneers. Such buildings were not uncommon on prairie homesteads, especially where wood was in short supply. Sod strips for the walls were often dug from sloughs, and poles covered with grass or hay fashioned a rather porous roof. Yet the thick walls of these crude shelters provided surprisingly good insulation from cold and heat. If you're in luck, hot bread might be emerging from a clay oven built outside the sod house.

North of Morrin, the terrain suddenly becomes hilly. This is classic knob and kettle topography, created when large ice sheets stagnated and disintegrated some 10,000 years ago. As the ice melted, it deposited large mounds of glacial debris separated by hollows. The result today is closely spaced hills with soils, wetlands and topography generally unsuited for cultivation. As a result, much of this area was untouched by the farmer's plough, which destroys native grasslands.

Aspen parkland is a transition zone between boreal forest to the north and prairie to the south. Rumsey is near its southern boundary on the plains. Aspen parkland is characterized by aspen forest in moist, sheltered areas and by fescue grasslands on drier, exposed areas such as hilltops and south-facing slopes.

The zone between grass and trees is a constant battleground for supremacy. In the Rumsey area, where some 70 per

The Rumsey Ecological Reserve protects part of one of the world's largest uninterrupted tracts of aspen parkland.

cent of the landscape is covered in grass, fires are believed to have helped limit the spread of aspen. In the past, natives often set fires to keep aspen and willow in check and to regenerate the grasses on which their main source of food, the bison, grazed. Where fire is suppressed, aspen will eventually reclaim lost territory.

The trees within an aspen grove often appear remarkably similar, both in size and in the timing of the greening and yellowing of their leaves. They are, in fact, clones. The roots of mature aspen produce suckers, which shoot out of the ground to become trees. Thus a considerable grove can arise from one parent root system.

The aspen in the Rumsey Ecological Reserve are relatively

short and grow in dense thickets, as anyone attempting to walk through one will discover. These groves provide excellent cover for sizable populations of mule and white-tailed deer and some sharp-tailed grouse. The reserve harbours several animal and plant species not commonly found in the area or the province. These include Baird's sparrow, upland sandpiper, sharp-tailed sparrow, the rare prairie vole and plants such as alkali bluegrass, American winter cress and spangletop grass.

At the north end of the reserve, there are a number of uncommon flat-topped hills that rise above the hummocky moraine. In the southwest area is a glacial spillway and eskers, which are serpentine ridges of gravel left by streams that once flowed under glacial ice. Other noteworthy habitats within the reserve are numerous wetlands, moist alkaline meadows and an ungrazed quarter-section in the southeast corner.

In the winter of 1793, Hudson's Bay Company explorer Peter Fidler passed through or near the area. This was an important wintering area, as the rolling terrain provided shelter for both the buffalo that roamed the plains and their Blackfoot pursuers.

With the disappearance of the buffalo and the signing of Indian treaties, this area became open rangeland in the early 1900s. The grazing rights were acquired in 1911 by the Calgary-based Burns empire, which relinquished its lease to Jim Walters and Tom Usher six years later.

The Usher family has been an excellent steward of the land. In 1990, more than 13 sections of their lease became the Rumsey Ecological Reserve. The reserve lands are still grazed but in a carefully managed fashion that ensures the native grasslands will be perpetuated. Please show the same respect when visiting the reserve to ensure the preservation of this small piece of a vanishing habitat.

Stettler Steam Train

ROUTE: From the Airport/Delacour Road overpass, drive 126 kilometres north on Highway 2 to the south end of Red Deer. Take Secondary 595 east for 45 kilometres, Highway 21 north, and Highway 12 east to Stettler. Alberta Prairie Steam Tours is located in the train station on the east side of Stettler.
DRIVING DISTANCE: About 210 kilometres one way.
NOTE: Alberta Prairie Railway Excursions operates old-fashioned steam train trips from Stettler from mid-May through October. Ticket purchases include a country dinner. For information and schedules, phone (403) 742-2811 or 290-0980 in Calgary.

In the 1920s and 1930s, the train was *the* way to travel through rural Alberta. The train carried passengers to the city,

Steam train pulling into Big Valley station.

mail and freight to distant destinations, and even hockey fans to a rival town for a Saturday night game. With all the stops to pick up passengers and freight, a rural run of only 80 kilometres might take nearly all day.

Today's frenzied urban dwellers can now experience that era of leisurely travel. Since 1990, Alberta Prairie Railway Excursions of Stettler has been offering a variety of day trips through central Alberta farmland, complete with country meals. Passengers can once again watch engine smoke billowing past the window, stick their head out between cars and feel the swaying, clickety ride as they head to the concession or bar car. The trip described below travels from Stettler south to Big Valley.

A steam train is a great way to see rural Alberta. Instead of focusing on a blurred white line, you're riding high on the rails as you pass close by open fields, aspen groves, sloughs and farmyards at a leisurely pace of about 35 kilometres per hour.

On a country train, wildlife is just outside the window. You're likely to see ducks, geese and perhaps tundra swans winging by, deer grazing, and hawks circling overhead. On a recent trip, I even saw a coyote chasing a red fox across a field.

An Alberta Prairie train is also a vehicle for a moving entertainment show. A couple dressed in cabaret finery passes through the cars, singing popular songs from early in the century. Train host "Gabriel Dumont"—with his long hair, scraggly beard and Sharps rifle—provides commentary on the passing countryside and a history of the great Metis leader he portrays. Dumont is usually called upon to apprehend masked and mounted bandits who halt the train and extract from passengers loose change, given to children's hospitals.

The train is an eclectic connection of a steam locomotive, two cabooses, and passenger, lounge and observation cars. Many were built around 1920 and served for decades on a variety of lines, including the southern United States, before being bought and restored for Alberta Prairie's use. On a full run, the string of coaches can extend more than 300 metres, one of the longest passenger trains in Canada.

The rail line on which these trips run was built in 1911 by Canadian Northern Railway as part of a branch line from Calgary to Vegreville, where it joined the Edmonton-Winnipeg main line. When Canadian Northern merged with the rival Grand Trunk Pacific Railway to form Canadian National Railway around 1920, the majority of north-south traffic shifted to the nearby Grand Trunk line to the east, though this line still carried passengers and freight.

Part of this money-losing stretch through Stettler was finally bought in the mid-1980s by Central Western Railway, a small company that still hauls grain and other commodities. Alberta Prairie was formed in 1990 to take over Central Western's passenger service, thus keeping this important tourist attraction alive.

While Stettler is enjoying the fruits of this fledgling railway, its vibrant economy still revolves around agriculture and, to a lesser extent, petroleum. It is a key commercial centre in east-central Alberta, providing business services to rural areas as distant as the Saskatchewan border.

The production end of this agricultural economy can be seen as the train chugs south past fields of wheat, barley, canola and hay. One reason for Stettler's long-standing success is that the valley's farmland has never experienced a crop failure. Much of the acreage is devoted to hay, which fuels a strong cattle industry. The Stettler area is known for its pure-bred strains, such as Charolais and Simmental, which are raised as seed stock and then cross-bred by beef producers elsewhere in Alberta.

Signs of the petroleum industry are soon passed as the train approaches Big Valley. A major oil field was discovered here in 1950, producing large quantities of oil and gas that are now largely depleted. The petroleum discovery replaced an earlier coal boom that once saw seven mines producing coal, primarily used for heating homes.

Big Valley, a pretty community of 300 residents nestled in a broad valley, is no stranger to booms and busts. At one time, it was a major divisional point on this rail line, supporting a population of more than 1,000 people. Locomotives were serviced and repaired here in a roundhouse, so-called because of its circular layout around a turntable. Today, the round-house is a concrete skeleton, with interpretive signs relating its glory days. Across the tracks, Big Valley's 1912 railway station has been lovingly restored to serve the new passenger train and to house a collection of historical photographs and community artifacts.

Reynolds-Alberta Museum

ROUTE: From the Airport/Delacour Road overpass at Calgary's northern outskirts, drive 220 kilometres north on Highway 2. Take the Wetaskiwin exit and drive 17 kilometres east to the Reynolds-Alberta Museum.
DRIVING DISTANCE: About 235 kilometres one way.
NOTE: The Reynolds Museum is open daily 10:00 a.m. to 6:00 p.m. from July 1 to Labour Day and 10:00 a.m. to 5:00 p.m. the rest of the year. Admission charged. Phone toll-free 1-800-661-4726.

The Reynolds-Alberta Museum is central Alberta's latest major tourist attraction and a shiny tribute to the machine age. Built around the collection of Wetaskiwin businessman Stan Reynolds, the $22.5-million facility features more than 100 restored artifacts ranging from ancient fire engines to vintage automobiles, many in working condition. Opened in 1992, the museum uses glossy exhibits, hands-on displays, videos and interactive computers to tell Alberta's history of mechanization in three areas—transportation, agriculture and industry. But above all, it is a monument to the car in Alberta.

■ Expansive views southwest from the lofty Leighton Centre, just south of Calgary.

■ Saturday crowds at the popular Millarville Farmers' Market.

■ Enjoying the view atop the 18,000-ton Big Rock near Okotoks.

■ Ranchers branding cattle near Maycroft along Highway 22 in southwest Alberta.

■ The Whaleback in southwest Alberta boasts Canada's largest and healthiest montane landscape.

■ Archaeologist Barney Reeves stands above the former bison-hunting cliff at Head-Smashed-In Buffalo Jump.

■ The Crowsnest River plunges over Lundbreck Falls just east of Crowsnest Pass.

■ The famous, and now dead, wind-sculpted Burmis Tree at the east entrance of Crowsnest Pass.

■ The High Level Bridge spanning the Oldman River in Lethbridge is the largest bridge of its kind in the world.

■ Trainer Stacey Steil rewards a Harris' hawk during a flying demonstration at Alberta Birds of Prey Centre, east of Lethbridge.

■ Fall aspen in the Ghost River Valley, northwest of Calgary.

■ The historic St. Ann Ranch, near Trochu, now a tea house and bed and breakfast.

■ A vibrant canola field in central Alberta.

The deeply eroded Red Deer River Valley at Dry Island Buffalo Jump Provincial Park.

You may think a two-and-a-half-hour drive on the immaculate pavement of Highway 2 constitutes an onerous day trip. But as you drive, consider what motorists endured at the beginning of the century, when the automobile was introduced to Alberta. Back then, roads followed old trails, railway allowances, ruts in farmers' fields and even creek beds. By the 1920s, the roads were usually good when dry but boggy or treacherously slippery when wet.

One solution, tried near Edmonton in 1923, was to apply a layer of bitumen to the road. The experiment worked but the cost of transporting the bitumen from distant oil sands near Fort McMurray was prohibitive. Instead, a gravel surface, graded and crowned to shed water, continued to be the easiest way to improve dirt roads. Many of these improvements resulted from the lobbying of early auto clubs such as the Alberta Motor Association, which also published the first road maps.

Despite such difficulties, the car provided unprecedented personal freedom and changed the way people lived and especially the way they played. The car opened the way for people to go to Banff or Sylvan Lake for weekend outings. It also led to the introduction in the 1920s of summer villages and of campgrounds, in which motorists slept in bungalow tents attached to the side of the car. These were hardly primitive outings. Campers often came equipped with folding chairs, tables, camp stoves and even portable phonographs. A later convenience was the bungalow camp, a forerunner of the motel, that featured a cluster of modest cabins around a central lodge.

These and other stories in the annals of the automobile industry are told at the Reynolds-Alberta Museum. Did you know that in the early years of the twentieth century, there was a race for supremacy between three means of powering motorized vehicles: steam, electricity and, the ultimate winner, the internal combustion engine? Indeed, Alberta's first recorded car was a steam-powered locomobile brought to the

Calgary area by William Cochrane around 1901.

There was also a battle for supremacy between the car and the horse. In Alberta, early automobiles were held responsible for all accidents with carriages. Later, they were still compelled to slow down or stop when passing horses. The first provincial motor vehicles act of 1906 restricted speeds to 10 miles per hour in settled areas and 20 elsewhere. And it wasn't until 1915 that cars were allowed into Banff National Park.

The real automotive boom came after World War II, when affluence descended to the middle classes and the province began a major road-building program. By 1955, there was one car for every five Albertans.

The Reynolds Museum relives that era by recreating period service stations, car dealerships and drive-in theatres. It also tells the parallel story of how agriculture was revolutionized by the gasoline-powered tractor and motorized truck.

Museum admission covers a visit to the adjacent Canadian Aviation Hall of Fame. Founded in 1973, the hall recognizes Canadians who have made a significant contribution to our aviation history. The hall's hangar displays 17 vintage aircraft including transport, sport, military and northern bush planes.

While in Wetaskiwin, you may wish to visit the city's pioneer museum and tour its historic downtown buildings. The word Wetaskiwin means "the place where peace was made." It refers to the legend of two braves from the warring Blackfoot and Cree nations who fought and then shared a peace pipe. Today, Wetaskiwin prides itself on being a city in motion, with the highest per capita car sales in Canada.

If time permits, it's worth returning to Calgary via the two-lane Highway 2A. Part of the original highway between Edmonton and Calgary, it is now a scenic back route that passes through Ponoka and Lacombe. This is a good opportunity to observe the fruits of the black clay loams rich in organic material. Here, wheat, barley, canola, grasses and forage crops are grown, and beef and dairy cattle raised. Situated on the banks of the Battle River, Ponoka features a wildlife sanctuary, a provincial building designed by renowned architect Douglas Cardinal and a leading hospital in brain injury treatment.

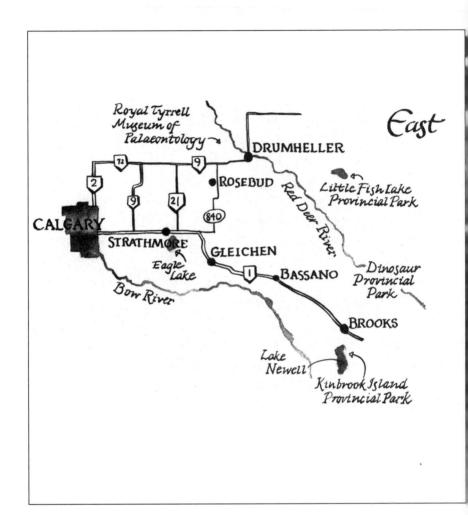

East of Calgary

The popular impression of the land east of Calgary is flat-as-a-pancake prairie. That impression no doubt dissuades many people from contemplating day trips east of the city.

Yet the prairies east of Calgary are surprisingly diverse and by no means flat. Anyone travelling east on the Trans-Canada Highway will soon realize these high plains are rolling. In many places, they provide panoramic views over a landscape that gradually becomes lower and flatter to the east and south. Even relatively flat stretches are periodically cut by draws and small drainages.

The most impressive landscape east of Calgary is the dramatic badlands of the lower Red Deer River Valley. Here, the forces of erosion have cut deeply through the exposed bedrock, creating a fantastic array of sculpted shapes. In sharp contrast to these desert-like lands are the nearby valley bottoms, which provide an oasis in the dry prairie for a diversity of plants and wildlife.

The two best places to see the badlands east of Calgary are in the Drumheller Valley and at Dinosaur Provincial Park, the latter a UNESCO World Heritage Site. Both contain rich deposits of dinosaur and other fossils. Many of these fossils are on display near Drumheller at the Tyrrell Museum of Palaeontology, one of the best museums of its kind in the world. Drumheller also offers the day-visitor two of Alberta's finest short driving loops, both packed with scenery and coal-mining history.

The other major destination east of Calgary is the Brooks area. Here, irrigation has transformed much of the short-grass prairie into productive farmland and created wetland habitats for many species of birds. Visitors to Brooks can visit a historic aqueduct, tour a pheasant hatchery or watch white pelicans and other birds at Lake Newell.

Despite the impacts of irrigated agriculture, there are still tracts of native mixed-grass and rough fescue prairie on the eastern plains. One of the best places to visit these is the Hand Hills Ecological Reserve, east of Drumheller.

Bird-watching Tour

ROUTE: From its intersection with Barlow Trail S.E., take Glenmore Trail/Secondary 560 east for 41.5 kilometres. Go 3.2 kilometres south on Secondary 817 and 5 kilometres east on a gravel road. Head 3.2 kilometres north on a rutted road past a small feedlot to a dead end overlooking the south end of Eagle Lake. To reach Namaka Lake, return to the east-west gravel road and drive 10 kilometres east along the north side of the lake. Turn south on a gravel road that passes a farmhouse to reach a dead end. A public parking area marked with "Buck for Wildlife" signs provides foot access to the lake.
DRIVING DISTANCE: About 70 kilometres one way.

The Calgary area is a bird-lover's paradise. The overlapping of three distinct ecosystems—fescue grassland, aspen parkland and foothills forest—provides a diversity of habitat for nesting and migrating birds. Add sloughs, alpine meadows and boreal forest within an hour's drive and it's easy to see why some 350 feathered species have been recorded in the greater Calgary area.

This tour of Eagle and Namaka lakes covers two of the area's best birdwatching sites. Because of their proximity to the city, both can be comfortably visited in a half-day's outing. Plan this trip for spring or late summer to mid-fall, when the

Canada geese preparing for fall migration.

influx of migratory birds fills the skies and wetlands. Try to reach the lakes in the early morning or evening, when birds are most active.

Carry a bird identification book, if you have one, and binoculars or a spotting scope. While any type of binoculars will do, a pair with a magnification of about 7 x 35 is recommended, especially for the distant viewing often required on lakes.

Heading east of Calgary, the city bustle quickly vanishes in the vast prairie landscape. These lands are part of the Western Irrigation District (WID), as is evident from irrigation canals and pivot sprinklers along the way. Water diverted from the Bow River within Calgary is fed east through a system of canals and reservoirs, including Eagle and Namaka lakes, to some 36,000 hectares of farmland. Unlike the dry prairie farther east, irrigation in the WID is more of an insurance policy than a necessity.

En route, a variety of winged predators can often be seen preening on fence posts, resting in treetops or circling high overhead in pursuit of unwary rodents or other small animals. The most common of these are Swainson's and red-tailed hawks, although the odd bald eagle and snowy owl might be spotted in winter.

From a hilltop 40 kilometres east of the starting point, Eagle Lake suddenly comes into view. It is one of the largest lakes in the Calgary vicinity and a prairie oasis.

Eagle Lake is no swimmer's paradise. The shallow water is murky brown and weedy. But it contains lots of nutrients for a variety of waterfowl and shorebirds. From the south end of the lake, those with persistence and a trained eye might also spot great blue herons, eared grebes, soras and terns. A marshy roadside slough near Eagle Lake Park along the east shore is also a good place to see numerous songbirds up close.

In fall, mallard and pintail ducks and Canada and white-fronted geese use the lake as a base for morning and evening forays into nearby fields of wheat, barley, oats and, surprisingly, peas. Essentially, they are carbo-loading for the long flight south. Geese prefer to land in summerfallow or ploughed fields and then walk into adjoining fields of harvested grain.

Although smaller than Eagle Lake, nearby Namaka Lake is one of the best places in the Calgary region for waterfowl and shorebirds, especially during the spring and fall migrations. An astounding 175 species of birds have been spotted here, including such treats as tundra swans, snow geese, sandhill cranes, common loons, white pelicans and American bitterns.

Nature has been aided by humans. Originally a smaller lake, Namaka increased in size early last century when the Canadian Pacific Railway started the irrigation system to lure settlers to lands east of Calgary. The pioneer conservation group Ducks Unlimited helped the cause in 1949 by building control structures and canals that resulted in more consistent water levels. More recently, an Alberta Fish and Wildlife project has further improved the bird habitat by planting trees and creating nesting islands.

From the parking lot, a grassy track leads down to the water on a neck of land that almost cuts the lake in two. Some of the best birdwatching is farther south, along the reedy shoreline.

Market Garden Tour

ROUTE: This is a design-your-own trip. To obtain a brochure listing market gardens in southern Alberta, phone toll-free 1-800-661-2642. Alternatively, simply drive east of Calgary a short distance on the Trans-Canada Highway and watch for U-pick road signs.

Not all fruits and vegetables come from grocery stores or farmers' markets. Indeed, the freshest produce one can find, outside a backyard plot, is within easy driving distance of the city. These are market gardens, where a variety of fruits and vegetables can be picked or bought straight off the vine. A tomato, strawberry or cob of corn never tasted sweeter than when plucked in its prime, rather than at the transportation convenience of a foreign agribusiness.

Purchasing produce at the farm gate is cheaper than at the supermarket, with all the proceeds going into the farmer's pocket. It's also an opportunity to see how the product is grown and what chemicals, if any, have been used. If nothing else, it's an excuse for a nice family outing into the countryside and a chance to chat with rural residents.

A trip to a market garden is also a means of replacing the losses from your own city garden. Despite its warm chinook winds in winter, Calgary has one of the worst climates in Alberta for growing vegetables, as anyone who has tried raising corn or tomatoes can attest. The reason is Calgary's high elevation (1,049 metres), which results in cool nights and frosts in late spring and early fall. I've lost more than one bean crop to an August snowstorm.

Most nearby market gardens are on small farms or acreages east of the city. The rolling farmland here is lower and slightly warmer than in Calgary, extending the growing season somewhat. True, these market gardeners don't enjoy the heat of Taber's corn growers to the south or the rich soils of Red Deer-area growers to the north. Most years, however, they produce abundant and diverse crops of vegetables and fruits.

The most common crop is strawberries, which I guarantee are sweeter than anything imported from California or Mexico. Other fruits are saskatoons, raspberries and tomatoes. Vegetables include peas, beans, carrots, potatoes, parsnips, lettuce, spinach, cucumbers, asparagus and onions.

The dozen U-pick market gardens just east and northeast of Calgary include Serviceberry Farms (934-2412), The Garden (936-5569), Blue Sky Gardens (934-2230), Poplar Bluff Farm (934-5400), Fray's Saskatoons (936-5413) and The Saskatoon Farm (938-6245).

The Alberta Market Gardeners Association publishes a brochure, *Come to Our Farms*, which lists member growers in Alberta. This brochure is available at many travel information offices or by calling the AMGA at 1-800-661-2642. There are also a number of non-member gardens. These are best found by keeping an eye out for market garden road signs on your rural travels.

Besides the area east of Calgary, there are also market gardens in the Okotoks and High River area and several around Olds and Bowden. One interesting place south of Olds is Rosebud Creek Herbs and Produce, where Peter and Jenny Reed specialize in fresh herbs (phone 556-1392; visits by appointment).

Although one can always drop in to market gardens, it's best to phone ahead. That ensures the owners will be home and the crop you seek is ready and hasn't temporarily been picked clean. The U-pick season is generally from early July until early September. If you can't make it to a market garden, you can often find the growers selling their produce at area farmers' markets.

Rosebud

ROUTE: From the intersection of 16 Avenue and 68 Street N.E. at the eastern outskirts of Calgary, drive 61 kilometres east on the Trans-Canada Highway. At the big bend in the highway, angle left onto Secondary 561 and follow it east for 7 kilometres. Turn north on Secondary 840, which leads to Rosebud in 31 kilometres.

DRIVING DISTANCE: About 100 kilometres one way.

NOTE: The Rosebud Dinner Theatre operates from spring until Christmas. All tickets are by reservation only. Phone (403) 667-2001 or toll-free 1-800-267-7553.

The Rosebud Opera House, one of many restored buildings in Rosebud.

This is a delightful trip through rolling countryside to the small town of Rosebud. Many Calgarians make this a full day's outing by attending the well-known Rosebud Dinner Theatre. But just getting there is at least half the fun.

The approach is on a quiet secondary highway northeast of Calgary. The road rises over hills etched with small draws and descends into intimate valleys containing slow-moving streams. Famed Canadian artists A.Y. Jackson and H.G. Glyde came to Rosebud in 1944 to sketch and paint the area's farms and ranches.

The lower valleys of the Rosebud River and its tributary, Serviceberry Creek, once contained fingers of Glacial Lake Drumheller. This huge lake was formed at the end of the last ice age, when glacial runoff was backed up by the retreating continental ice sheet. When the lake drained, it left broader, flatter valleys behind.

The Blackfoot called the river *Akokiniskway*, the "river of many rosebuds." The name refers to the profusion of wild roses, Alberta's provincial flower, that appear along the river's banks in June. Serviceberry Creek, which joins the river just west of Rosebud town, is named for the wild, delicious saskatoon berries, also called serviceberries, that ripen in summer in the river valleys.

Aboriginal peoples came to these valleys to pick berries, fish and seek shelter from winter storms. In the surrounding hills, they hunted the buffalo, which once covered the mixed-grass prairie in vast numbers. In 1792, Hudson's Bay Company surveyor Peter Fidler witnessed native people stampeding buffalo to their death over a steep cliff along the Rosebud River.

This area was long the domain of the Blackfoot. When a hunting party of Cree entered this Blackfoot territory around 1860, they were decisively beaten in a bloody combat at Battle Hill, south of Rosebud near Severn Creek. In the early 1950s, Severn Creek was dammed to control flooding and erosion and to provide water for downstream cattle. The resulting reservoir, 10 kilometres south of Rosebud, is now a popular place for picnicking and fishing for stocked trout.

In the winter of 1875, Methodist missionary John McDougall travelled east from his mission at Morleyville to the open country around Rosebud in search of buffalo. But, by then, the vast herds of buffalo had been nearly wiped out. Two years later, the Blackfoot, deprived of this life support and decimated by white diseases, signed Treaty No. 7 and thus relinquished their claim to these lands.

That paved the way for settlers. The first was the Wishart family, who camped here in 1885 en route to a new home in Montana. Captivated by the area's beauty, they never left, building a log house on a homestead along the Rosebud River.

In the ensuing years, Rosebud became a thriving community of farmers and ranchers. The big boost was the completion of the national Canadian Northern Railway's line between Drumheller and Calgary. This so-called Goose Lake Line stopped at Rosebud, where several elevators were erected to transport grain to distant markets. A number of coal mines also operated in the area, the last closing in the mid-1960s.

Today, tourism and the arts are supplementing the area's agricultural economy. Several of Rosebud's turn-of-the-century buildings have been restored and converted to new uses. The Rosebud Centennial Museum is housed in an old Chinese laundry, the Akokiniskway Gallery in a Presbyterian church, the Rosebud Opera House in a converted grain bin, and the Rosebud School of the Arts in a mercantile building.

The School of the Arts is a post-secondary Christian school that focuses on theatre arts. It also operates a popular non-denominational dinner theatre, attracting audiences from a wide area.

Drumheller

ROUTE: From the Airport/Delacour Road overpass, drive north on Highway 2 for 26 kilometres. Take the exit and follow Highway 72 east, which beyond Beiseker becomes Highway 9 leading to Drumheller. It's well worth stopping at Horseshoe Canyon, 8 kilometres before Drumheller, for a good introduction to the badlands landscape.

DRIVING DISTANCE: About 125 kilometres one way.

NOTE: Drumheller can also be reached by driving east of Calgary on the Trans-Canada Highway and then heading north up a choice of Highways 9, 21, or Secondary 840. The last two offer perhaps the most scenic approaches.

The dinosaurs are long gone. So, too, more recently, are the coal mines. But their stories are told in the museums, relics and even soft rocks of the Red Deer River Valley that cuts deeply through the Drumheller area. It is the combination of natural features and history that makes the Drumheller Valley one of the most compelling destinations in Alberta.

The big draw, of course, is the Royal Tyrrell Museum of Palaeontology, opened in 1985 and attracting hundreds of thousands of enthralled visitors each year. But the museum is only a lure to the other worthy attractions of the Drumheller Valley. There are hoodoos, old coal mines, a stretch of eleven narrow bridges, a cable ferry and native prairie grasslands. The most compelling feature of all is the severely sculpted bad-lands of the Red Deer River Valley.

It's easy to get overwhelmed or overscheduled on a day trip to the Drumheller area. The best bet for the day tripper is to visit the museum and take one of the two short driving tours described here. The alternative is to stay overnight in one of the numerous campgrounds and motels in the area. If you have many visiting relatives and friends, chances are you'll be making more than one trip to Drumheller anyway, so you can divide the attractions into manageable pieces.

Drumheller

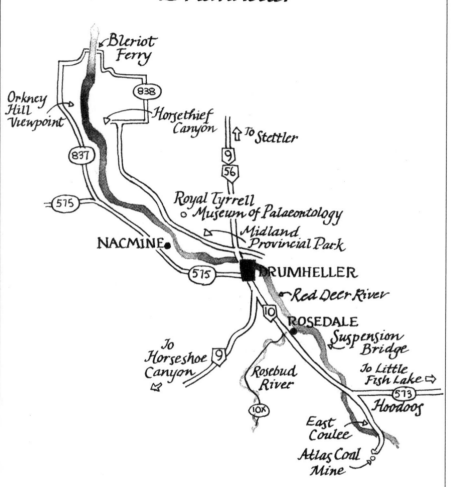

Drumheller is named after Samuel Drumheller, an American entrepreneur who, in the early twentieth century, registered the sixth of 138 coal mines that once operated in the valley. Actually, the city could easily have carried the name of an earlier homesteader, Thomas Greentree. He lost a coin toss with Drumheller to see what the town should be called when the first post office opened in 1911.

Once well known for its jail, Drumheller is now awakening to its tourist opportunities. It boasts a growing number of small, private museums, rock and fossil shops and even a living Reptile World. This small city of 6,300, nestled in the flood plain of a deep valley, also makes its living from the bread and butter industries of agriculture and oil and gas services.

Royal Tyrrell Museum of Palaeontology

ROUTE: The museum, located within Midland Provincial Park, is 7 kilometres west from downtown Drumheller on secondary Highway 838, the Dinosaur Trail.

NOTE: The museum is open daily 9:00 a.m. to 9:00 p.m. from Victoria Day to Thanksgiving weekend, and from 10:00 a.m. to 5:00 p.m. Tuesday through Sunday the rest of the year. Admission charged. Phone (403) 823-7707.

The Royal Tyrrell Museum of Palaeontology is arguably the finest dinosaur museum in the world. The $30-million facility, which opened in 1985, contains dozens of complete dinosaur skeletons, as well as many audiovisual presentations and hands-on displays. For example, visitors can design their own dinosaur on a computer terminal.

Tyrrell is more than just a celebration of dinosaurs. Befitting a museum devoted to palaeontology—the study of ancient life through fossils—it chronicles 3.5 billion years of the earth's history, of which the dinosaur era was a significant snapshot. It is also a major research facility, where excavated fossils are studied, preserved and, in many cases, prepared for display.

As one of Alberta's most popular attractions, the Tyrrell is crowded with "dinophiles" throughout the summer. The best bet is to arrive at 9:00 a.m. sharp or in late afternoon or early evening, when the crowds have thinned somewhat. Expect to spend three or more hours touring the exhibits. Those with young children might consider limiting the time spent in the introductory sections and concentrating on the dinosaur displays.

The museum's name honours Joseph Burr Tyrrell, a renowned geologist with the Geological Survey of Canada, who, in 1884, discovered the first dinosaur remains, an albertosaurus skull, in the Drumheller area. On the same trip, Tyrrell also noted the coal deposits in the Drumheller Valley. Both his discoveries eventually provoked rushes—for coal and dinosaur bones. Incidentally, the "Royal" in the title commemorates a British royal visit after the museum opened.

The museum tour begins with a recent discovery of fossilized dinosaur eggs in southern Alberta and a hands-on display of how things like levers, pulleys and laws of science work. Beyond, the displays are in chronological order, proceeding from the universe's origins and the first forms of life through early vertebrates, reptiles and, finally, mammals.

The highlight, of course, is the 150-million-year age of dinosaurs. In the dinosaur hall, one can gaze in wonder at 130-million-year-old fossilized footprints, dinosaur eggs and magnificent skeletons of such creatures as the carnivorous Albertosaurus and the duck-billed Edmontosaurus. The Burgess Shale exhibit depicts a 500-million-year-old underwater world, complete with a glass floor. The showstopper is still the immense and toothy Tyrannosaurus rex, the largest of the meat eaters and one of the last dinosaurs in this area.

Many of these skeletons were unearthed from ancient rock

formations in the Red Deer River Valley, particularly around Drumheller and in Dinosaur Provincial Park, 140 kilometres downriver. The latter's dinosaur beds are rivalled only by sites in China's Gobi Desert.

The dinosaur's world was closer to today's Florida coast than the dry, rocky Red Deer Valley we now see. Seventy million years ago, this was a warm, lush environment on the edge of an inland sea. Dinosaurs roamed through swamps and marshes, eating the abundant vegetation or, if carnivorous, other creatures. An approximation of this environment can be experienced by visiting the museum's palaeoconservatory. It contains many prehistoric plants, including some that trace their ancestry back 350 million years.

What led to the relatively sudden demise of the dinosaurs some 65 million years ago? There's still no conclusive answer. Some scientists believe it was caused by a gradual change in climate, while others lean to the catastrophic consequences of a huge meteorite impact. It is instructive to realize there was a much larger extinction of species prior to the dinosaur era. In fact, some 99 per cent of all species that have ever lived on the earth are thought to be extinct.

While the museum provides a gripping account of the dinosaur era, the surrounding valley also reveals millions of years of history to the observant. It's a good idea to escape the glassy-eyed indoor crowds and venture up to a viewpoint overlooking the badlands. Better yet, take a short, interpretive walk into the badlands from near the museum's entrance. This trail provides a close-up look at the various layers of ancient silts, sands, muds and plants compressed over the millennia into stratified rocks and coal deposits. These rock layers erode rapidly, occasionally exposing their long-buried treasures of dinosaur bones. Note: Do not disturb or remove any fossils you may encounter.

Dinosaur Trail

ROUTE: The route is well marked throughout as the Dinosaur Trail. From down-town Drumheller, cross the Red Deer River on Highway 9. Turn west on Secondary Highway 838, which follows the river's north side. The route crosses the river at the Bleriot Ferry and loops back along the south side of the valley to Drumheller.

DRIVING DISTANCE: About 47 kilometres return.

The Dinosaur Trail packs a lot of history and natural features into 47 kilometres as it follows a looping course along both sides of the Red Deer River. Indeed, it is one of the best short driving tours in Alberta. To do it justice, allow at least two hours.

Horsethief Canyon.

The tour begins by passing the Homestead Antique Museum, which contains thousands of historic items including aboriginal relics and turn-of-the-century pioneer clothing and machinery. Just beyond is Midland Provincial Park.

The park visitor centre is housed in the 1912 office building of the Midland Coal Mine, a once-thriving operation that closed in 1959. The building contains historic photos and a thick, brick-walled vault that secured a payroll delivered by armed guards. The best of several nearby interpretive walks is the #2 Mine trail, which circles the grassed-over remains of an old mine site. In the mine's early years, the coal was hauled in cars from the seam by Shetland and Welsh ponies.

Across the road is McMullen Island, an oasis of greenery in the otherwise parched badlands. On a hot day, it's a good spot for a picnic, particularly if you've spent the morning hours in the nearby Royal Tyrrell Museum of Palaeontology. As you drive into this day-use area, notice the sharp transition from desert-like to riverine vegetation. The dry sagebrush gives way to poplars, tall cottonwoods and, finally, thick clumps of sandbar willows along the banks of the Red Deer River. The luxuriant growth here is made possible by deposited silts in the broad, flat part of a river valley that elsewhere is eroded into steep banks. This island of vegetation attracts deer, rabbits and a number of songbirds.

Just beyond the Tyrrell Museum is the roadside Little Church, a non-denominational place of worship and meditation that seats six. Originally built by a local contractor in the late 1960s, it was reconstructed by inmates of the Drumheller federal penitentiary in 1991.

The ensuing stretch of road alongside the golf course provides a good view of the stratified layers of sandstones, mudstones, ironstones and coal seams that make up the badlands. Near the road are small scattered rocks that were carried here thousands of years ago by glacier from as far away as the Precambrian Shield of the Northwest Territories. Some of these rocks—particularly those of granite, gneiss or schist—could be more than 2 billion years old.

The road climbs to a plateau overlooking the Red Deer River. In surrounding fields, pumpjacks are rhythmically lifting a mixture of oil, gas and water from rock formations some 1.5 kilometres below the surface. The gas in this field is sour, meaning it contains deadly hydrogen sulphide gases. With more than 3,000 active oil and gas wells within a 50-kilometre radius of Drumheller, it's not surprising that energy servicing is the area's second-largest industry, behind agriculture.

The importance of ranching is evident in the name of a spectacular viewpoint, Horsethief Canyon. In the past, horses apparently lost in the maze of badland gulleys below would often reappear sporting different brands. While horses and cattle now graze in nearby fields, the prairie grasses that once flourished here were home to vast herds of bison as well as the now extinct plains grizzly bears and wolves. The wildest creatures one might see now are the more adaptable deer and coyotes.

An ancient form of life, oysters, are preserved in a large fossilized rock at the Horsethief Canyon lookout. They are a 67-million-year-old legacy of a vast sea that once covered this now arid landscape.

The road soon drops steeply to the Red Deer River, which is crossed on the Bleriot Ferry, one of the last remaining cable-operated ferries in Alberta. The small ferry, now gas-powered, previously made the short voyage by pointing its nose upstream and, with the aid of channel boards, allowing the current to carry it across. The ferry is named after André Blériot, who homesteaded near here in 1902. He built and, for many years, operated the ferry. He was overshadowed, however, by brother Louis Blériot, who, in 1909, became the first person to fly a plane across a much bigger body of water, the English Channel.

Along the far side of the river is the Bleriot Ferry

Campground. Cottonwoods and willows grow by the river; farther inland are native prairie grasses and wildflowers. Some of the area's first dinosaur bones were discovered nearby in the 1880s. That sparked the Great Canadian Dinosaur Rush of the early twentieth century, in which internationally renowned scientists scoured the Red Deer Valley for fossilized dinosaur remains.

As the route leaves the river flats, the prairie grasses give way to stands of white spruce, which grow on the cooler and wetter north-facing slopes of the valley. Back on top of the plateau, it's a short drive to yet another magnificent lookout, Orkney Hill Viewpoint. This high perch provides a clear view of how the river has cut its ever-shifting channel out of the soft banks. The higher terraces above the current flood plain are former riverbeds, abandoned when periods of high water flow cut a new and deeper channel.

Like a roller-coaster, the road drops again to the flood plain and crosses several brackish streams. Despite their diminutive size, these streams have travelled many kilometres from the northwest to empty into the Red Deer River. The final stretch of road passes Nacmine (short for North American Collieries Mine) and Newcastle, two early coal-mining towns on the outskirts of Drumheller.

East Coulee Drive

ROUTE: From its junction with Highway 9 in southeast Drumheller, follow Highway 10 east for 22 kilometres to the Atlas Coal Mine. Return the same way, taking a 7-kilometre detour en route from Rosebud to Wayne via Highway 10X.
DRIVING DISTANCE: About 60 kilometres return.
NOTE: The East Coulee School Museum and Cultural Centre is open daily from 9:00 a.m. to 5:00 p.m. in the summer, and for reduced hours the rest of the year. Phone (403) 822-3970. The Atlas Coal Mine Museum is open daily, 10:00 a.m. to 6:00 p.m., Victoria Day to Labour Day. Admission charged. Phone (403) 822-2220.

One of 11 single-lane bridges on the short road to Wayne.

East Coulee Drive is another of the fine short driving tours in the Drumheller area. It is primarily a tour into the rich coal-mining history of the Drumheller Valley. Along the way are opportunities to stretch your legs on a long suspension bridge and to stroll up to hoodoos sculpted by wind and water.

As you drive along this route, it's easy to see why coal mining was the dominant industry in this valley for the first half of the century. The dark, narrow layers in the badland rocks are seams of coal, formed by the compression and transformation of swamp-like vegetation that grew here along the coast of an inland sea some 70 million years ago. Of the 11 identifiable coal seams in the valley, only four were commercially mineable.

Peter Fidler noted these exposed coal strata while leading a Hudson's Bay Company expedition through the area in 1793. Nearly a century later, geologist Joseph Burr Tyrrell (for whom the nearby museum of palaeontology is named) redis-covered the valley's abundant coal deposits. Early settlers burned lumps of the coal in their stoves. But it wasn't until the Canadian National Railway arrived in 1911, providing access to Canadian markets, that a coal boom erupted.

Within a few years, more than 40 mines were operating in the Drumheller Valley, creating instant towns and prosperity. The coal was used to heat homes and the coal dust com-pressed into briquets to power steam railway locomotives. With the big oil discovery at Leduc, near Edmonton, in 1947, the demand for coal slumped and most of the valley's remain-ing mines closed soon thereafter. The Atlas Coal Mine, at the end of this tour, was the last to go, ceasing operations in 1979.

Relics of old mines and still-smouldering heaps of coal slag are evident along this drive. Just past Rosedale, one can walk on a 117-metre suspension bridge across the Red Deer River to the abandoned Star Mine, which operated from the mid-1910s to 1957.

If you think this swaying walk is exciting, consider the early miners who crossed the river first in rowboats, then in aerial cable cars. The suspension bridge was constructed in 1931 and rebuilt and upgraded by the Alberta govern-ment—after the mine closed—to allow the safe passage of vis-itors.

The next stop, 7.5 kilometres beyond the bridge, is the Hoodoos Recreation Area, where you can inspect the forces of nature on the rock pillars across the road. Hoodoo, a variation of voodoo, was the European word for these fantastically shaped formations. The Blackfoot and Cree had a more vivid sense of the pillars, believing them to be petrified giants who came alive at night to hurl rocks at intruders.

Hoodoos are formed when a cap of hard sandstone pro-tects the softer underlying rock from eroding as rapidly as the surrounding rock. The result is a free-standing pillar of sand-stone on a thick base of shale. Once exposed to wind and water, hoodoos will erode away in a few thousand years. Geologists believe these particular pillars could be gone in a hundred years, a process perhaps accelerated by thoughtless people clambering all over the site.

It's another 5.4 kilometres to the entrance to East Coulee. This hamlet was, in the 1930s and 1940s, a boom town of 3,500 people, many of them immigrants from Hungary and the Ukraine who worked in six area coal mines. The East Coulee School Museum and Cultural Centre has preserved that era through exhibits, a 1930s school classroom, a tea room and a gift shop.

Beyond East Coulee, the Atlas Coal Mine is reached by crossing a narrow trestle bridge, which once served cars and trains. The mine, a provincial historic site, contains the last standing ore-sorting tipple of its kind in the entire country. This large wooden structure stored sorted coal in bins for loading into boxcars and trucks bound for distant markets. The mine closed in 1979 and is being restored as a coal complex and interpretive centre, which can be toured.

Return on Highway 10 to the small town of Rosedale, once the site of the largest coal mine in the Drumheller field and drive south on Highway 10X. Over the next 7 kilometres, it crosses eleven single-lane bridges over the meandering Rosebud River, named *Misaskatoomina Sipisis* by the Cree for the abundant saskatoon bushes in the narrow valley. Many of the original timbers for these bridges were floated downstream from Red Deer on the Red Deer River.

During its heyday, the Rosebud Valley near Wayne boasted six operating coal mines and a population of 2,000 people. Today, Wayne is a hamlet whose claim to fame is as a location for such films as *Running Brave* and *2001: A Space Odyssey.* Wayne obviously prides itself on its independent spirit. It features a motorcycle ranch, a store boasting no GST and a real western bar, The Last Chance Saloon.

Hand Hills

ROUTE: From its junction with Highway 9 in Drumheller, drive 15.5 kilometres east on Highway 10. Turn left on 573, a good gravel road that leads in 25 kilometres to Little Fish Lake Provincial Park. The Hand Hills Ecological Reserve is best accessed by driving north from the park on Secondary 851, west for 5 kilometres on Secondary 576, and then south on a dirt road to the reserve boundary, marked with signs.

DRIVING DISTANCE: About 45 kilometres one way from Drumheller.

NOTE: Although the Hand Hills Ecological Reserve is on Crown land, leaseholders graze cattle on the site. Please respect these operations as well as the fragile natural habitat.

Little known or advertised, the Hand Hills contain one of the largest intact tracts of fescue grassland in the world. Considering native prairie grasslands are among the most threatened habitats in the world, a visit to the Hand Hills Ecological Reserve is a rare opportunity. A picnic lunch at Little Fish Lake Provincial Park and a short drive north into the heart of the Hand Hills makes a nice half-day outing from Drumheller.

Most people imagine the terrain east of Drumheller to be flat and low-lying. Thus, it is surprising to encounter the Hand Hills, the second-highest point in Canada between the Rocky Mountains and the east coast. A thick gravel cap has protected these hills of sandstone and shale from repeated glacial erosion, leaving them standing up to 185 metres above the surrounding prairie.

The Hand Hills cover a circular area extending north from Little Fish Lake to near Delia. The topography is undulating and cut by numerous steep-sided drainage valleys. The views of the rolling prairie and deep Red Deer River Valley are superb from these heights.

Established by the province in 1988, the Hand Hills Ecological Reserve protects 2,229 hectares of land near Little

Fish Lake. The reserve is in the northern fescue zone, a prairie grasslands sub-region unique to Canada's prairie provinces. Its ecosystems include rough fescue grasslands, alkaline seepage areas, seasonal sloughs, moist meadows and aspen groves.

Much of Canada's fescue grasslands has been lost to agriculture. Once the fragile soils are turned by the plough, the native grasses are lost forever. Intensive cattle grazing can also disturb this native prairie beyond repair.

The ecological reserve's native prairie is still largely intact because it has been neither ploughed nor intensively grazed. A management plan is being devised for the Hand Hills reserve to allow for some continued grazing while preserving the natural habitats. But this area is still vulnerable to further damage.

As you stand amid the reserve's swaying grasses, try to imagine this landscape as white explorers would have seen it 200 years ago. Back then, the native prairie stretched to the horizon on rolling hills. Native hunters frequently set up tipis in these high hills, gaining extensive views over the surrounding prairie. According to legend, the Hand Hills are named for a Blackfoot warrior with a withered hand who died during a battle here with the Cree.

Today, perhaps the most immediate sensation for visitors is made through the feet. Unlike a planted field or urban lawn, the native prairie ground is uneven, crunching underfoot as you gingerly walk over it. It's a bit like tramping around the hummocky edge of a slough. If you get down on your hands and knees, you'll discover the layer above the dark brown soil consists of tiny plants such as club mosses, mosses and lichens.

Arising from these clumps are a variety of grasses, principally rough fescues, which grow in large clumps up to 50 centimetres tall. Because these fescues are fairly sensitive to grazing, secondary grasses such as porcupine, June and wheat grasses become more dominant in disturbed areas. Blue grama grasses and low sedges are found on more heavily grazed sites.

Among the reserve's profusion of summer wildflowers are rare and uncommon plants including crowfoot violet, stiff-yellow paintbrush, mountain shooting star and, along the lakeshore, small-flowered evening primrose. Aspen groves and shrubs are found in sheltered draws.

The reserve's wildlife includes sharp-tailed grouse, thirteen-lined ground squirrels, prairie long-tailed weasel, badgers, coyotes, mule deer and such threatened or endangered species as Baird's sparrow, ferruginous hawk and peregrine falcon. The 10,000-year-old fossilized bones of prairie dogs have also been found in the Hand Hills. During the last interglacial period, they created extensive networks of tunnels beside rivers. A species of gregarious burrowing rodents, prairie dogs are no longer found in Alberta.

Little Fish Lake, which cuts into the eastern boundary of the ecological reserve, was once a popular destination for fishing and boating. Though the lake has receded considerably in recent years, the provincial park at its southeast corner still attracts a number of campers. The park contains a number of archaeological sites, where tipi rings and campsites have been discovered.

The piping plover nests along the gravelly shores of Little Fish Lake. An endangered species in Canada, this small shorebird has been adversely affected by human and livestock travel along the beach. Thus, the province and conservation groups have erected shoreline fences and discouraged pedestrians from using the beach during critical nesting periods.

To reach the height of the Hand Hills, take the scenic drive north of Little Fish Lake on Secondary 851. Just south of Delia is Mother's Mountain, which offers a panoramic view over the prairies. Return to Drumheller via Highways 9 west and 56 south.

Calgary to Brooks

ROUTE: From the intersection of 16 Avenue and 68 Street N.E., at Calgary's eastern outskirts, drive 176 kilometres east on the Trans-Canada Highway to Brooks.

The route from Calgary to Brooks and Medicine Hat is on the heavily travelled Trans-Canada Highway and follows the Canadian Pacific Railway (CPR) main line. Yet it is perhaps the most recent of the major transportation corridors in Alberta.

While fur traders, explorers and whisky traders established a network of trails elsewhere, an east-west route across the southern prairies was ignored until the late nineteenth century. The major reason for this was the stranglehold the Blackfoot Nation held over these lands for many years.

The arrival of the North-West Mounted Police in 1874 ended the illegal whisky trade with the Indians. But already hard hit by white diseases and the decimation of the buffalo, the Blackfoot, led by Chief Crowfoot, signed Treaty No. 7 at nearby Blackfoot Crossing in 1877. Several years later the Blackfoot—who, along with the Blood and Peigan, comprised the Blackfoot Nation—moved onto their reserve near Gleichen, just south of the Trans-Canada Highway. A small museum on the third floor of the Old Sun College in Gleichen tells the story of what is now known as the Siksika Nation. Call (403) 734-3862.

Despite the arrival of the railway in the early 1880s, this route remained largely undeveloped for the next two decades. Only the periodic railway sidings and the odd store disturbed the prairie skyline between Calgary and Medicine Hat. All that changed when irrigation was introduced to this dry landscape, attracting settlers and prompting towns to pop up.

The impact of irrigation is visible all along the Trans-

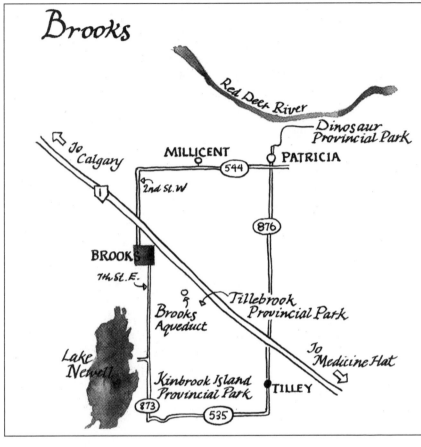

Brooks

Red Deer River

Dinosaur Provincial Park

To Calgary

MILLICENT

544

PATRICIA

2nd St. W

876

BROOKS

7th St. E.

Tillebrook Provincial Park

Brooks Aqueduct

To Medicine Hat

Lake Newell

Kinbrook Island Provincial Park

TILLEY

873

535

Canada from Calgary to Brooks. Just beyond the city limits, the highway passes the burgeoning community of Chestermere Lake. In 1910, the lake became a reservoir for storing water diverted from the Bow River at Calgary. Eagle Lake, just east of Strathmore, is also part of this network of canals and man-made reservoirs in the Western Irrigation District, east of Calgary. Here, irrigation is largely an insurance policy against dry summers.

The rolling farmland east of Calgary has been largely shaped by glaciers that periodically covered southern Alberta for much of the past 2 million years. The road crosses an end moraine, a ridge of rock deposited by melting glaciers, at a rise of land just before Cluny.

From such panoramic high points, the eastern horizon begins to expand and flatten. But this is by no means the bald prairie of popular belief. The landscape continues to roll, albeit more gradually, and is cut by many small valleys. At about 110 kilometres, the deep Bow River Valley becomes visible as it parallels the highway before swinging south to join the South Saskatchewan River.

When Captain John Palliser passed through this area during his prairie reconnaissance of the late 1850s, he described desert-like conditions unfit for farming. In all, these arid lands became known as Palliser's Triangle, an area containing much of southwest Saskatchewan and southeast Alberta. Yet a look at today's County of Newell map reveals a prairie oasis dotted with lakes, sloughs and other wetlands. Virtually all these bodies of water have been created by irrigation.

The source of this transformation can be viewed by taking a 10-kilometre detour south at Bassano to the Bassano Dam on the Bow River. Completed in 1914, the dam created a reservoir that now provides water, through a network of canals, to some 110,000 hectares of irrigated farmland and six communities.

This system is a legacy of the CPR, which was granted vast tracts of land in the 1880s as part of its agreement to build the national railway. The CPR introduced irrigation to these semi-arid grasslands around 1910 as a means of attracting settlers and building a viable farm economy. But the railway lost money operating the system and in 1935 turned its lands and irrigation infrastructure in this area over to a farmer-owned co-operative, the Eastern Irrigation District (EID).

Today, the EID is the largest irrigation district in Canada, encompassing more than 600,000 hectares, an area bigger than Prince Edward Island. Of that total, the district owns some 245,000 hectares of rangeland, making it the largest private landowner in Alberta. Large numbers of cattle are grazed on these lands and also raised in feedlots. Given the abundant supply of land and easy access to Canadian and international markets, via the CPR main line and Trans-Canada Highway, it's not surprising the cattle industry is king here. You can smell the prosperity as you pass feedlots close to Brooks.

Brooks

For a prairie town of 10,000 people, Brooks has a surprising diversity of attractions. Indeed, the area's variety of things to see and do may be unmatched outside Alberta's major cities.

The biggest draw is nearby Dinosaur Provincial Park, a World Heritage Site and one of the finest depositories of fossilized dinosaur bones in the world. It's just one of three provincial parks near Brooks, the others being Tillebrook and Kinbrook Island. The latter is a fine place to watch birds, particularly the graceful white pelican. Brooks also boasts a historic aqueduct and a horticultural research centre.

Given its distance from Calgary, it's best to pick a couple of attractions for a day trip. The best bets are Dinosaur and Kinbrook provincial parks and the Brooks Aqueduct. The alternative is to stay overnight at a motel or one of the fine provincial park campgrounds and explore the area at your leisure.

Dinosaur Provincial Park

ROUTE: From the Trans-Canada Highway on the western edge of Brooks, follow the Dinosaur Provincial Park signs for 48 kilometres north and east on paved secondary highways.

NOTE: The park Field Station, which has an interpretive centre, is open daily 8:30 a.m. to 9:00 p.m. from May 15 to Labour Day, and on a shorter schedule the rest of the year. Park tours are offered from May until October. Phone (403) 378-4342 for more information.

Dinosaur Provincial Park contains one of Alberta's most fascinating and diverse landscapes—the severely eroded badlands. Here, one can find fantastic rock shapes, stands of plains cottonwood trees, cacti and prairie rattlesnakes. Perhaps most importantly, it boasts one of the most abundant sources of fossils in the world. Not surprisingly, this unique park is a UNESCO World Heritage Site.

Much of the park is closed to personal explorations. Thus, the best way to see its treasures is to take a tour or a self-guided interpretive walk near the visitor centre.

Dinosaur Provincial Park contains the largest tract of badlands in Canada. A pull-off near the park entrance provides an excellent overview of this landscape. The term "badland" is a translation of *mauvaise terre*, a description early French traders applied to a similar landscape in North Dakota. Badlands are largely barren areas in which soft rock strata have been rapidly eroded by water and wind into steep slopes and varied, fantastic forms.

About 14,000 years ago, torrential meltwaters from retreating glaciers began to deeply carve this stretch of the Red Deer River Valley. Today, 100 metres of sedimentary bedrock have been exposed from the level prairie to the valley bottom, revealing a geological timeline. As the river's murky colour shows, this rapid erosion continues today, washing away sands, silts and muds deposited millions of years ago.

The harsh badlands are a far cry from the flat, semi-tropical world that existed here 75 million years ago. This was a coastal plain near the eastern edge of an inland sea. Ferns, mosses and other lush vegetation grew here, supporting a diversity of plant- and meat-eating dinosaurs.

The dinosaurs disappeared about 65 million years ago, but their legacy was preserved. During the dinosaur era, rivers from young mountains to the west deposited thick layers of sands, silts, muds and clays that encased and eventually preserved many bones as fossils. Over time, these deposits were compressed into horizontal layers of sandstones, mudstones, shales and ironstone.

These are the layers of the badlands, which are eroding away at a rate of about 4 millimetres per year. The badlands' loss is the palaeontologist's gain. The rapid erosion has unearthed many fossilized remains of dinosaurs and other animals and plants. Indeed, Dinosaur Provincial Park is the world's most abundant source of fossils from the late Cretaceous period. To date, more than 35 species of dinosaurs have been discovered here.

The Drumheller-based Royal Tyrrell Museum of Palaeontology maintains a field station here, where scientists continue to make exciting discoveries. Recent excavations include skeletons of the huge, carnivorous Albertosaurus, the duck-billed hadrosaur and the rarely found pterosaur, a flying reptile with a wingspan exceeding 6 metres. These fragile specimens are painstakingly removed and preserved. Many are prepared for display in the park or at the Tyrrell Museum.

Incidentally, scientists can accurately date these dinosaur remains but not from the fossils themselves. Instead, they examine the volcanic ash in the rock layers containing the fossils. The ash, deposited during the dinosaur era, is preserved in thin green clay beds called bentonites. Anyone driving these roads after a rainstorm will soon be acquainted with the slippery properties of bentonite clays.

While the badlands are themselves largely sterile, the valley is by no means devoid of life. In fact, it contains rich ecosystems of sharp contrast. The Red Deer River is a natural oasis in the dry, mixed-grass prairie of southeast Alberta. This stretch of the river is home to one of the greatest concentrations in Alberta of plains cottonwoods. These giants, some more than 200 years old, provide nesting sites, shelter and insect food for a variety of birds. Unfortunately, the annual spring flooding needed to establish new generations of cottonwoods has been affected by an upstream dam. This habitat can be viewed by following the short, self-guided Cottonwood Flats Trail along the river.

The river bottom and shaded tributary valleys also support dogwood, willows, saskatoon bushes and small birch trees. In the morning and evening, thirsty deer and coyotes might be seen along the river's edge and cottontail rabbits along park roads. During the day, predators such as ferruginous hawks, golden eagles and prairie falcons might be seen riding thermal air currents high above.

Away from the river, the environment is desert-like. Here, amongst the sagebrush and cactus, the inhabitants include prairie rattlesnakes, scorpions and black widow spiders. While venomous, these desert creatures are generally shy, their bites rarely fatal. Chances are, most park visitors will never see them.

Brooks Aqueduct

ROUTE: From the tourist information building on the eastern outskirts of Brooks, drive 3 kilometres south of the Trans-Canada Highway on a dirt road to reach the aqueduct.

NOTE: The site's interpretive centre is open daily, 10:00 a.m. to 6:00 p.m., from May 1 to Labour Day. Admission charged. Phone (403) 362-4451.

When it opened in 1915, the Brooks Aqueduct was the longest structure of its kind in the world. Today, this concrete skeleton is a national and provincial historic site and an elegant testimonial to a marvel of engineering.

In 1912, the challenge for the Canadian Pacific Railway was to build an aqueduct that would span a 3.2-kilometre valley and carry water from man-made Lake Newell to the eastern lands of this irrigation district. The problem was complicated by the need to maximize the water flow without losing much elevation.

The engineering solution was to build a unique, dish-shaped concrete flume supported by more than 1,000 columns. In less than three years, a crew of 300 men had completed the aqueduct, using as much concrete as it would take to build some 630 house basements. It is now considered one of the 10 greatest engineering achievements in Alberta's history.

The aqueduct brought agricultural fertility to some 55,000 hectares of farmland for 65 years. But, as the years passed, the badly deteriorating concrete structure could no longer keep up with the rising demand for water. In 1979, it was replaced by an earth-fill canal capable of carrying nearly 50 per cent more water. While utilitarian, the canal is visually insignificant next to the classical symmetry of the concrete dinosaur that stretches off into the prairie distance.

Kinbrook Island Provincial Park

ROUTE: From Brooks, drive 13 kilometres south on Secondary Highway 873 and 2 kilometres west to reach Kinbrook Island Provincial Park.

Kinbrook Island Provincial Park is a small "island" that extends on a strip of land into the eastern waters of Lake Newell. The 38-hectare park features two campgrounds, picnic areas, a sandy beach, warm water swimming, a boat launch and irrigated trees and shrubs that provide shade from the summer sun. It is also one of the best bird-watching areas in southeast Alberta.

Covering 7,100 hectares, Lake Newell is the largest man-made lake in Alberta. Fed by waters diverted from the Bow River at the Bassano Dam, the lake is an important storage reservoir for irrigating large tracts of otherwise arid grassland. It was created in 1914 by flooding a low-lying area within two large coulees and diking eastern runoff areas.

Flooded trees along the edge of Lake Newell.

Dams have often been rightly criticized for destroying or significantly altering the surrounding habitat. While irrigation has transformed the dry prairie landscape, Lake Newell and nearby irrigation wetlands have created an oasis in southeast Alberta for more than 100 species of birds.

The lake is the summer home of Alberta's largest colony of double-crested cormorants and a sizable breeding population of American white pelicans. The white pelican, a threatened species in Alberta, nests on aptly named Pelican Island in the southwest corner of Lake Newell. With a weight of up to 8 kilograms and a wingspan of more than 2 metres, the pelican is one of the largest birds in the world. Rather gawky looking on land or water, it soars elegantly when airborne.

Boats are not allowed within 1.6 kilometres of Pelican Island so as not to disturb these sensitive birds. But boaters can angle elsewhere in this deep lake for whitefish, northern pike and rainbow trout. A commercial whitefish fishery has been in operation on Lake Newell since 1936.

Fish and birds are not the only treasures of Lake Newell. Approximately a kilometre beneath the surface are pools of oil trapped in rock reservoirs that millions of years ago were sandy river islands and bars. These oil deposits are currently being tapped by wells drilled on an angle from the lakeshore.

Given the lake's size, it can be difficult to watch birds from shore. Fortunately, nature lovers can get much closer to a diversity of birds at Kinbrook Marsh, along the edge of Kinbrook Island Provincial Park. This former shallow bay was separated from Lake Newell by three dikes in 1988, creating a permanent marsh full of reeds, cattails and willows. This is one of a number of wetland projects undertaken by the Eastern Irrigation District in partnership with Ducks Unlimited and Alberta Fish and Wildlife.

An interpretive trail, complete with a viewing platform and powerful scope, has been developed around the north marsh. An evening stroll along the edge of this rich habitat might reveal Canada geese, mallard ducks, shy American bitterns, great blue herons, pelicans and even the great horned owl. In the shallows might be lurking muskrat, beaver or mink.

The marsh borders on another important ecosystem, the mixed-grass prairie. While irrigated agriculture has converted much of the native prairie in this region to cropland, large tracts of grazing land are still in a fairly natural state.

These hardy prairie grasses are well adapted to tolerate infrequent rainfall, extreme cold, drying winds and drought. Their branched roots form dense tangles that absorb moisture and nutrients and hold the soil together. Narrow leaves and a thick protective layer also conserve water. Since the grasses grow from their base, they can be grazed, cut, trampled, or burned and continue to grow. But ploughing kills them.

With luck, you might spot the magnificent ungulate of the treeless plains—the pronghorn, or antelope as it is commonly called. Almost wiped out at the turn of the twentieth century by agriculture and hunting, the pronghorn's numbers have rebounded to about 15,000 in the province. On the open prairie, pronghorn can reach speeds of 95 kilometres per hour. But unlike deer, they are not jumpers. Indeed, they usually crawl under barbed wire fences.

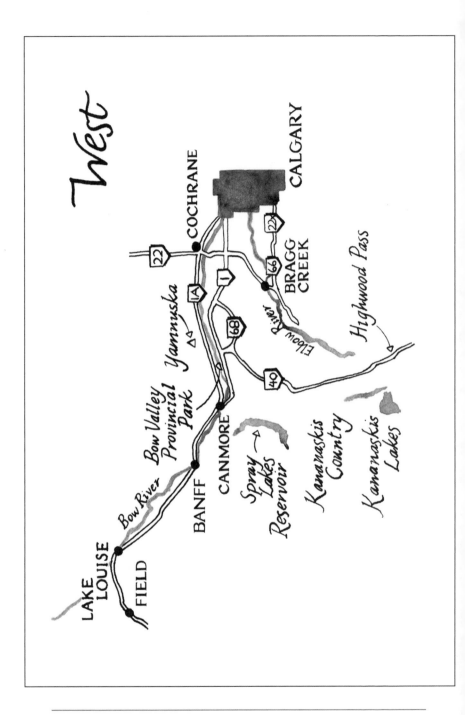

West of Calgary

Veteran Calgary travellers might think they know all the attractions west of the city. After all, they may have travelled dozens, if not hundreds, of times to the mountains.

But have they discovered the charms of Bow Valley Provincial Park, which contains one of the most diverse ecosystems in Alberta? Have they detoured off the Trans-Canada Highway to visit the Sibbald Creek area and its wealth of ancient history? Have they ventured into an old prisoner-of-war camp along the Kananaskis Highway? Have they walked above the hoodoos in Banff or wandered up the narrow valley of Heart Creek? Do they know that the first large-scale ranch in Alberta was located west of the city?

There is, then, much to discover west of Calgary that is not in the glossy mountain brochures. Even the drive west on the busy Trans-Canada Highway and the not-so-busy 1A Highway can reveal much about the landscape and the area's history to those willing to look beyond the pavement and beckoning peaks.

The Bow River Valley is the central corridor for trips in this section. The river arises from near the Wapta Icefield, north of Lake Louise, and follows a broad, glacially carved route through the mountains and onto the plains. This corridor contains the major highways, towns and tourist attractions west of Calgary. The Bow Valley funnels the chinook winds that warm the winter valley and create unique ecosystems. It also contains the Canadian Pacific Railway, which, through an aggressive advertising campaign and the construction of two major hotels, unveiled the mountains as an international tourist destination in the late nineteenth century.

The other destinations in this section follow tributaries of the Bow River. One trip follows the Elbow River out of Calgary and into the low mountains west of Bragg Creek. Two others head south along the Kananaskis and Spray valleys, where visitors can engage in numerous recreational activities or simply marvel at the impressively folded mountains, formed tens of millions of years ago.

There are also trips into the tourist meccas of Banff and Lake Louise. With a little effort, it is possible to take short walks that quickly leave the camera-clicking and shopping bag-toting hordes behind. Even heavily visited Lake Louise still maintains a majestic splendour a century after it was unveiled to an awestruck world.

Cochrane

ROUTE: From the western terminus of Bow Trail at a T-intersection, turn north and follow Old Banff Coach Road as it bends west out of Calgary. From Coach Hill Road S.W. (0 kilometres), continue west, angling right at 4.2 kilometres to stay on Old Banff Coach Road, which crosses the Trans-Canada Highway at 10 kilometres. Turn west on a road that passes Springbank Airport en route to a junction with Highway 22. Follow Highway 22 north to its intersection with Highway 1A. The Cochrane Ranche is on the right.
DRIVING DISTANCE: About 35 kilometres one way.
NOTE: The Cochrane Ranche visitor centre is open daily, 10:00 a.m. to 6:00 p.m., from May 15 to Labour Day. The grounds can be visited at any time of the year. Phone 932-1193 or 932-2902.

Cochrane is a lovely town with sweeping views of the nearby foothills and mountains. Now a bedroom community of Calgary more focused on raising children than cattle,

Cochrane was once known as a cattle centre. Indeed, it is the birthplace of large-scale ranching in western Canada. This tour passes through modern ranch and farm country en route to Cochrane and its shrine to early ranching.

Old Banff Coach Road seems a misnomer for a narrow highway that peters out en route to Cochrane and has no history as a stagecoach route. Yet, in the late 1800s, this was an alternative approach to the mission at Morley and the mountains beyond. Travellers would head west from Fort Calgary, following the open prairie on the south side of the Bow River, which could be crossed at several places between Cochrane and Morley. It was used primarily in winter when the main route west (the current 1A Highway) was covered in snow.

In 1909, Norman Lougheed initially followed the Banff Coach Road route when he made the first car trip from Calgary to Banff. He drove in two deep wagon ruts through Springbank, crossing the Bow River on the Cochrane Ferry.

Looking up Big Hill Creek Valley from Cochrane Ranche.

Not far beyond the current city limits, he would have passed the dairy farm of Ebenezer Healy, who built the area's first cheese factory in 1888.

Today, acreages increasingly cover Springbank, but there are still a number of small farms, where horses and cattle can be seen grazing. One of the biggest of these operations is Rudiger's, which raises the distinctive white Charolais cattle alongside the Trans-Canada Highway.

This rural-urban mix continues on the north side of the Trans-Canada as the road passes a housing development and then a stable with a small equestrian course. The Calgary area can lay fair claim to being the horse capital of Canada. Many acreage owners maintain a horse or two for riding, adding to a population of diverse breeds raised for show or to herd cattle. Not surprisingly, Canada's largest dude ranch, the 1,800-hectare Griffin Valley Ranch is just west of Cochrane.

The road continues west through farmland and past the small but busy Springbank Airport. Just before the Highway 22 junction, the road climbs to a hilltop offering a magnificent panorama of mountains. From here, it's a short drive north to the Bow River and Cochrane, where a sign announces the town is a "nuclear weapons free zone."

On the northwest edge of Cochrane is the Cochrane Ranche Provincial Historic Site, a monument to a grand failure in nineteenth-century ranching. In 1881, Quebec Senator Matthew Cochrane obtained from the Canadian government the first of the 100,000-acre (40,470-hectare) ranching leases in southern Alberta. For the annual sum of 1 cent per acre, these ranch owners could graze cattle on grasslands once roamed by the buffalo.

In two great cattle drives, nearly 12,000 animals were herded from Montana to Cochrane's ranch along the banks of the Bow. Alas, many animals were lost to successively harsh winters and poor management. By 1883, the Quebec businessman had moved his cattle south to a new lease near Cardston that eventually prospered. The Cochrane operation briefly experimented with sheep- and then horse-ranching. In 1890, much of its lease was relinquished to provide land for homesteaders.

Today, visitors can tour a 62-hectare historic site that once contained a manager's house, a bunkhouse, a blacksmith shop and a stable. During the ranch's operation, well-heeled managers would arrive at their quarters with pianos, polo ponies and fine china, while hired hands lived in leaky barracks.

The visitor centre contains artifacts of this era and provides a brief history of ranching in the area. Interpretive programs and special events are offered in late spring and summer. Even when the visitor centre is closed, you can walk up the hill to the impressive bronze statue of a rancher on horseback, designed by local artist Malcolm MacKenzie. This perch overlooks the town of Cochrane and provides a magnificent view of the mountains, the most prominent of which is Devil's Head.

Perhaps the best part of the visit is to continue walking north up through the valley of Big Hill Creek. A short trail loops from the statue back to the visitor centre through a surprisingly diverse landscape. The right side of the valley faces north and receives little direct sunlight. Thus, its moist slopes are thickly covered with white spruce and aspen and an understorey of mosses. The exposed left side features sandstone outcrops, prairie grasses and a profusion of wildflowers fed by springs seeping down the hillside. Beaver dams in the creek bottom have created a wetland that attracts a number of bird species.

The Big Hill Valley was carved into its U shape by melting waters from an early ice age. These meltwaters emptied into the nearby Glacial Lake Calgary, an ice-jammed lake that covered the Bow Valley from Calgary west to Morley. Today, Big Hill Creek winds from Big Hill Springs Provincial Park, to the north, through the ranch and Cochrane to empty into the Bow River. Those with sufficient time can follow a nice trail along the creek to the river.

Halfway up the left side of the Big Hill Valley is the Western Heritage Centre, a museum that honoured the livestock and rodeo industries. At the time of publication, the financially strapped centre was closed.

While in Cochrane, it's worth visiting the downtown area, sampling the famous MacKay's ice cream or perhaps heading to Studio West to watch western bronzes being made.

Elbow River Tour

ROUTE: From the traffic lights on Sarcee Trail just south of Richmond Road S.W., follow Highway 8 west for 22 kilometres to a T-intersection. Go 37 kilometres south on Highway 22 past Bragg Creek to another intersection. Follow Highway 66 west to its terminus at Little Elbow Campground.
DRIVING DISTANCE: About 90 kilometres one way.

This trip traces the Elbow River upstream for much of its length, transporting visitors from high plains through forested foothills to low mountains. Along the way are opportunities to view riverine habitats, overlook a fine waterfall and take an alpine hike. This is a good afternoon outing or evening picnic destination that can easily be extended to a full day.

In 1814, explorer David Thompson mentioned an east-flowing river that turned sharply north at an "elbow." The river he described is the Elbow River, its abrupt turn occurring at what is now Glenmore Reservoir in southwest Calgary. Fed by this modest river, the reservoir collects sufficient water to meet nearly half the city's needs.

The Elbow River is thought to be millions of years old. During the formation of the Rocky Mountain front ranges, it

Hiker ascending Nihahi Ridge.

continued its eastward journey, carving its way down through the gradual uplift of bedrock. Today, the Elbow still carves through the bedrock, exposing a timeline of rock layers that can be seen at such places as Elbow Falls.

The wider Elbow Valley was sculpted into a U shape thousands of years ago by glaciers advancing east out of the mountains. Parts of the upper valley, however, apparently escaped the brunt of the last ice age, creating an ice-free corridor for migrating animals and early native hunters. Near the Bragg Creek valley, there was once a glacial lake—an arm of the larger Glacial Lake Calgary—fed by meltwaters from the Elbow River and Jumpingpound Creek.

In more recent times, the Elbow region was the overlapping hunting grounds of the Sarcee, Peigan and Stoney people. The Stoney Trail, a major trading route along the foothills between Rocky Mountain House and Fort Macleod, passed through the Bragg Creek area.

The Sarcee, now known as the Tsuu T'ina, own lands south of Highway 8 and on both sides of Highway 22 leading to Bragg Creek. Their economic developments along the latter include the Redwood Meadows golf course and several hundred adjacent housing units purchased by non-natives.

Early white visitors to the area included Father Constantine Scollen, who, in 1873, erected the first church in southern Alberta, the Mission of Our Lady of Peace. The mission was moved two years later to the fledgling Fort Calgary. A cairn marks the site of the original mission—a crude cabin 12 kilometres north of Bragg Creek near Highway 22. Sam Livingston, one of the first white settlers in the Calgary area, later built a trading post near the mission site.

In the 1890s, ranching and coal mining arrived in the Elbow Valley. Bragg Creek is named after Albert Bragg, an early rancher who was initially a squatter. Because of earlier fires, the first settlers often did not have to clear land to start their farms and ranches. Ironically, much of this open land is now covered in trees.

Today, Bragg Creek is a bustling community nestled in coniferous forest at the base of the foothills. On weekdays, acreage owners commute to Calgary. On weekends, tourists arrive en masse from the city to visit the shops, restaurants and numerous galleries. Most, however, fail to venture beyond the retail centre to explore the natural beauty of the upper Elbow Valley.

By heading west on Highway 66, one can stop at numerous spots along the Elbow for picnics and riverside walks. A good interpretive walk, 8 kilometres west of the visitor centre, is Paddy's Flat. This 2.2-kilometre trail follows an old river terrace through forest and then loops back along the edge of the Elbow River.

These terraces were formed during periods when a swollen river cut rapidly through glacial gravel deposits to form a new channel, leaving the previous one high and dry.

■ Restored turn-of-the-century buildings, including a classic flatiron building, in downtown Lacombe.

■ Hoodoos in evening near Drumheller.

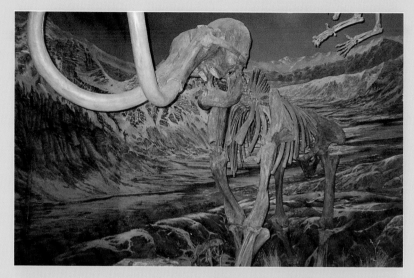

Dinosaur exhibit at Royal Tyrrell Museum of Palaeontology near Drumheller.

Jumpingpound Creek on a side road south of the Trans-Canada Highway west of Calgary.

The south face of Mount Kidd, along Highway 40, in Kananaskis Country, offers a classic example of rock folding.

Fall cycling on paved pathway south of Ribbon Creek in Kananaskis Country.

Photo: Travel Alberta

■ Majestic golden eagles make a major migration twice a year along the front ranges of the Rocky Mountains.

■ Yellow lady's slippers make their showy spring appearance along the Many Springs Trail in Bow Valley Provincial Park, west of Calgary.

■ A brilliant display of autumn alpine larch in the upper Pocaterra Valley near Highwood Pass in Kananaskis Country.

■ The south face of Yamnuska, in the front ranges west of Calgary, is a limestone cliff that attracts rock climbers from around the world.

A Parks Canada interpretive hike along Vermilion Lakes near Banff townsite.

The blue-green waters of Grassi Lakes, above Canmore.

■ Moraine Lake and the Valley of Ten Peaks near Lake Louise.

■ Guided hikers ascending to the Burgess Shale fossil beds above Emerald Lake in Yoho National Park.

Over thousands of years, a sequence of these steps formed, descending to the current riverbed. The old terraces now support a diversified forest, with fast-growing lodgepole pine and aspen on the sunny flats and white spruce and poplars along the edges of a spring-fed stream.

The most popular stop along the river is at Elbow Falls, 5.4 kilometres beyond Paddy's Flat. A 400-metre paved path (wheelchair accessible) leads to a viewpoint overlooking the falls. Here, the river has been funnelled into a gap in the exposed bedrock, where it plunges over a rock step into a foaming pool. In a few centuries, however, the constant battering of water on rock will have reduced these falls to rapids.

The road beyond Elbow Falls is closed from December 1 to May 15. In summer and fall, continue west as the highway climbs to Rainy Creek Summit and descends to Little Elbow Campground, where the Elbow and Little Elbow rivers join. En route are impressive views to the southwest of Mount Glasgow and Banded Peak. Along with Mount Cornwall, these peaks retain their snow cover through much of the year and are thus easily seen from Calgary.

If time and energy permit, the 3-kilometre hike up to Nihahi Ridge is well worth the considerable effort. The trail is reached by proceeding to the far end of the campground, walking along an old fire road for about 500 metres, and then turning right and following the Nihahi Ridge signs. The trail climbs steeply through a thick stand of lodgepole pine, which shelters the white spruce that eventually will succeed it. South-facing clearings are ablaze with wildflowers such as Indian paintbrush and brown-eyed Susan.

The trail swings left across a grassy bowl, dotted with wind-stunted trees, and climbs onto a ridge with stellar views of the Elbow Valley and peaks to the south and west. It is possible to continue ascending the ridge on a fainter and narrower trail, but the loftier views are perhaps not worth the additional exertion.

Sibbald Creek Loop

ROUTE: From the Canada Olympic Park traffic lights, drive 35 kilometres west on the Trans-Canada Highway. Take the Sibbald Creek Trail exit and follow Secondary Highway 68 south and then west for 37 kilometres to Highway 40, which is followed north to the Trans-Canada and back to Calgary.
DRIVING DISTANCE: About 140 kilometres return.

This tour of the forested foothills 45 minutes west of Calgary has something for everyone—excellent birdwatching, trout fishing, camping, interpretive hiking and native history. The only thing missing is wilderness. Logging, natural gas exploration, cattle grazing and even target shooting are also allowed in this eastern section of Kananaskis Country, aptly called a multiple-use area. Still, this is a fine foothills introduction, often bypassed by motorists heading for the mountains.

Serious birdwatchers often flock to the wetlands along Sibbald Creek Trail, where in spring and summer up to 50 species of birds may be spotted through binoculars. The birding begins in a small slough to the right of the Sibbald exit off the Trans-Canada Highway. In late March to early April, this pond is a good place to see migrating trumpeter swans and the occasional tundra swan. The trumpeter swan, named for its bugling call, has a wingspan of more than 2.5 metres. Considered threatened in Alberta, this elegant, long-necked bird makes a brief spring appearance en route to northern breeding grounds, primarily in the Grande Prairie area.

Heading south on Highway 68, you will soon pass a series of wetlands fed by runoff from surrounding hills. The sloughy waters, grasses, willows and nearby tree cover provide excellent habitat for a diversity of birds. Patient and timely viewers might see red-winged blackbirds, lesser yellowlegs, common snipe, red-winged hawks, yellow warblers and pine siskins, to name a few.

At 5 kilometres, the road rises to a hilltop with a commanding view of thickly forested foothills. The underlying bedrock of these foothills consists mainly of relatively young layers of sandstone and shale. These soft rocks have readily eroded into rounded hills covered with layers of till deposited by glaciers. The soils are primarily leafy humus over sandy clays, typical of a forest environment.

The forest here is primarily coniferous, with white spruce covering cooler, moister north-facing slopes and lodgepole pine and some aspen on drier south-facing slopes. Not surprisingly, such healthy stands have attracted logging since the turn of the century. In past years, even the local citizenry has come here to fell lodgepole pines for Christmas trees.

Visitors can learn about Alberta's forest management practices by visiting the Jumpingpound Forest Interpretive Centre, 5 kilometres past the Kananaskis Country boundary. A 10-kilometre interpretive drive from the centre stops at various places that have been logged and replanted.

Just beyond this interpretive drive is Sibbald Viewpoint, a lofty spot overlooking an expansive meadow. These grassy flats are named after the area's first rancher, Frank Sibbald, who introduced longhorn steers to the grasslands in 1890, 15 years after his family settled here.

The human history of this area goes back to the end of the ice age, when the first inhabitants roamed the area in pursuit of bison, woolly mammoths, and even camels. Archaeologists have unearthed several nearby prehistoric campsites containing bison bones and stone tool fragments, some 10,000 to 11,000 years old.

The Stoney people still consider these foothills a spiritual area. For years, they have performed Sun Dances, an annual summer ceremony banned under the Indian Act from 1885 to 1951. The remains of Sun Dance lodges—small aspens arched into the rounded shape of a sun—can often be seen in a meadow along the Sibbald Flat Trail, a 1-kilometre interpretive loop from Sibbald Lake.

Another worthwhile hike from Sibbald Lake is Ole Buck Loop. This 2.4-kilometre loop trail climbs to a high point offering views of the lake below and Moose Mountain on the horizon. But perhaps the highlight is a lovely, mature stand of poplar that shelters a dense growth of cow parsnip. From the viewpoint, the trail drops steadily to grassy slopes that overlook the willowy meadows and beaver ponds of Bateman Creek.

Just beyond Sibbald Lake, Sibbald Creek Trail passes the north end of Powderface Trail. This summer gravel road provides access to excellent ridge walks along its east side. When passable, it also leads to the Little Elbow Campground and Highway 66 to Bragg Creek.

Still heading west, the paved Sibbald Creek Trail gives way to a good gravel surface as it enters a narrower valley cloaked in thick coniferous forest. Industrious beavers have created a series of willowy ponds along Sibbald Creek, attracting anglers casting for rainbow and brook trout. The fishing pressure is heavier at nearby Sibbald Meadows Pond, which has a parking lot and picnic tables.

A nicer and quieter picnic spot is reached by driving a few kilometres farther along the steadily descending road to Lusk Creek, fringed in early summer with fragrant wolf willow and yellow dryads. From Lusk Creek, it's a short drive to the junction with Highway 40.

Bow Valley Provincial Park

ROUTE: From the Canada Olympic Park traffic lights, drive 65 kilometres west on the Trans-Canada Highway. Take the Bow Valley Provincial Park exit and head north for 800 metres, turning left to reach the visitor centre and most of the park.

DRIVING DISTANCE: About 65 kilometres one way.

NOTE: For information on Bow Valley Provincial Park, call the park at (403) 673-3663.

On perhaps my two-hundredth trip west to Banff's mountains, I finally pulled off the Trans-Canada Highway and discovered the jewel that is Bow Valley Provincial Park. There, within earshot of the racing traffic, is an understated park containing one of the richest ecosystems in Alberta. Actually, it's a meeting place of three zones—mountains, grasslands and boreal forests—with two rivers and a spring-fed marsh adding to the biological diversity.

Consider that such disparate birds as bald eagles, rufous hummingbirds, meadow larks, ruffed grouse and harlequin ducks can all be at home in this 935-hectare park. Or that this is the only place in the world where the tiger salamander of the prairies and the long-toed salamander of the mountains breed in the same location. During a leisurely hour's walk, one can spot dozens of wildflower species, including such showstoppers as lady's slippers, western wood lilies and elephant's heads.

The task, then, is not finding points of interest, but determining how to fit it all in. A good plan is to visit often and digest a bit at a time. At less than 45 minutes from Calgary, this is a perfect destination for a picnic supper and interpretive walk during the long evening hours of early summer. Indeed, the park is perhaps best seen in June and early July, when the flowers are at their peak.

Between 1902 and 1930, this site was just inside the eastern boundary of an expanded Banff National Park. Once that protection was lost, to allow industrial development in the Canmore area, cattle grazing and rock quarrying ensued. Finally, in 1959, Bow Valley Provincial Park was established. Today it is bisected by the Trans-Canada Highway and bounded on two sides by the merging Bow and Kananaskis rivers. It also forms the northern portion of Kananaskis Country.

The best way to explore Bow Valley Provincial Park is through its six interpretive trails, each unveiling a different aspect of the park's treasures. All but one can be reached from the paved road that winds down to the Bow River, where visitors can picnic alongside grazing Canada geese. Park brochures are available at the visitor centre.

Following is a sampling of the trails. But first, a suggestion to park officials. Please erect at the park entrance a large sign that says: **Do not pick the flowers!** It is illegal to pick flowers in a provincial park and highly destructive to do so in an area that contains many rare species. I once saw a young woman happily displaying a bouquet of freshly picked wood lilies. Once these beautiful orange flowers are picked, the plant dies.

Many Springs Trail

This 1.6-kilometre trail, near the west end of the park, circles an unusual, spring-fed wetland. Because the water temperature stays at a constant six degrees Celsius, a variety of animals and birds can be found here year-round. Elk and deer are also attracted by the minerals in the spring water. One interesting plant found along the water's edge is elephant's head, which on close inspection does resemble a column of purple elephant trunks. Another interesting inhabitant is a form of isopod, a tiny blind creature with a 400-million-year-old ancestry, which lives in underwater darkness.

Montane Trail

This 1.5-kilometre walk from the visitor centre explores the transition from prairie to forest. In the open meadows, ground-hugging plants are well adapted to surviving the strong, drying chinook winds. The trail then follows an esker—a serpentine, and now grassy, ridge of gravel left by streams that once flowed under glacial ice. The homeward loop passes through a mature forest that includes a magnificent stand of Douglas fir. These ancient giants perhaps owe their longevity to their thick, fire-resistant bark.

Flowing Water Trail

This is a 1.4-kilometre tour of sharp contrasts. The trail begins in a cool, forested terrace intersected by iron-rich streams descending to the Kananaskis River. (While scenic, the river is largely barren, thanks to regular releases of water from an upstream dam that have scoured the river bottom.) It then climbs a grassy slope of wildflowers to an exposed hilltop, where strong winds have produced a dry climate and stunted trees. Farther along, nature's developer, the beaver, has fashioned dams, blocking the flow of small streams and creating an extensive marshland. Compare this to the nearby handiwork of human developers, who some decades ago built hydroelectric dams on the Kananaskis and Bow rivers. The trail is reached from the far end of the campground on the east side of Highway 1X.

Kananaskis Valley

ROUTE: From Canada Olympic Park traffic lights, drive 61 kilometres west on the Trans-Canada Highway and exit onto Highway 40; follow it south for 50 kilometres to its junction with the Kananaskis Lakes Trail. Stop at the Barrier Lake visitor centre, 7 kilometres south on Highway 40, for information and brochures.

DRIVING DISTANCE: About 120 kilometres one way.

In theory, this should be a short day trip. After all, it's little more than an hour of straight driving from the city limits to the end point of this tour. Yet so much scenery, history and recreational and educational opportunities are packed into this 50-kilometre stretch of the Kananaskis Valley, a full day only scratches the surface. Consider this description, then, as a menu for a brimming buffet table, from which visitors can pile their plates as they choose. Second, third and fourth helpings are recommended, at suitable intervals.

Highway 40 initially crosses the windswept Morley Flats that were once the bottom of a glacial lake. This lake was formed when melting icewaters from high in the Kananaskis Valley were blocked by an arm of the large Bow Valley glacier. When the glaciers receded about 10,000 years ago, the lake was drained.

Not long after, the first recorded humans entered the valley. These ancient ancestors of the Kootenai often spent their summers around Boulton Creek, close to Kananaskis Lakes. They followed bison and elk down-valley to the shelter of winter camps at nearby Wasootch Creek and the Bow River. By the mid-1700s, the Stoney had driven the Kootenai west across the mountains and claimed the valley for hunting and fishing.

But their tenure was short-lived. The arrival of white explorers in the mid-1800s, followed by prospectors, trappers and the like resulted in forest fires, overhunting of elk and the near extermination of the bison. After the Stoney signed Treaty No. 7 in 1877, they moved to their Bow Valley reserve, part of which extends across the flats and into the forests along Highway 40.

In this century, white development has subdued the Kananaskis River through a series of hydroelectric dams. The river, once called Strong Current by native peoples, now flows mostly tranquilly alongside the highway. Two beneficiaries of this development are canoeists and kayakers, who take advantage of the daily release of water from the upstream Barrier Dam to practice their whitewater skills. You can often see them performing their manoeuvres by walking down to the river from the Canoe Meadows parking lot, 5.5 kilometres from the Trans-Canada Highway.

A few kilometres farther, Barrier Lake and Dam come into view. The dam opened in 1947, creating a reservoir with a capacity of 25 billion litres. For a commanding view of the lake and the Kananaskis Valley, drive another 2.3 kilometres to a picnic area, where a short interpretive trail climbs to a hilltop.

Much of the tree clearing and earth moving for the Barrier Dam was performed by German prisoners of war held captive at a nearby camp during World War II. At first, the camp held male Germans living in Canada as well as German merchant seamen captured overseas at the outbreak of war. Later, captured German soldiers were brought here, including some who fought under Erwin Rommel's command in North Africa. Though the prisoners were apparently well treated, they lived in a camp fenced by barbed wire and overlooked by towers manned by armed guards with searchlights.

In summer, visitors can tour one of the guard towers and the Colonel's Cabin, the former camp commandant's office and now a provincial historic site. To reach them, turn left at the Kananaskis Forest Experiment Station, 2.5 kilometres past the visitor centre.

Behind the cabin are two connected interpretive trails (2.3 kilometres in length) that explain the mixed forest's ecology and forest management practices. One stop is at a small pit, where visitors can observe the four layers of soil that sustain this forest environment. For four decades, these lands were the site of a federal forest research station. The scattered survivors of one experiment—to plant non-native species such as Norway spruce and jack pine—can be seen along the far loop. The forest research station has been replaced by the University of Calgary's Environmental Science Centre.

The limestone cliffs along this section of the valley attract a number of rock climbers. These athletes can often be seen from the road, scaling the steep walls below Barrier Mountain. The slabs along nearby Wasootch Valley are one of the most popular training areas for climbers in the Canadian Rockies.

Just beyond Wasootch Creek are the Mount Lorette Ponds. A former bend in the Kananaskis River cut off by highway construction, these small ponds were dredged, stocked with rainbow trout and ringed with paved trails. This is a popular family picnic and fishing spot, which is wheelchair accessible. There are also several nearby beaver ponds containing rainbow and brook trout. For more information, ask at a visitor centre for the *Fishing in Kananaskis Country* brochure.

Coming into view on the right is Mount Allan, the home of Nakiska Ski Resort and site of alpine skiing events at the

1988 Winter Olympics. Its selection over rival candidates in the valley to the west was controversial due to its proximity to wintering bighorn sheep and reliance on snow-making equipment. Mount Allan overlooks a cluster of other tourist and sporting developments near Ribbon Creek, including the three hotels of Kananaskis Village, a 36-hole championship golf course and a deluxe RV park complete with satellite television hookups.

Visitors to the Ribbon Creek area can also hike or cross-country ski on a network of trails. This is the starting point for a lovely, paved cycling trail that winds south through forest along the highway for 7.3 kilometres to Wedge Pond.

The Ribbon Creek area is no stranger to development. The forests here were logged in the late 1930s and early 1940s and the timber trucked out of the Kananaskis Valley via a forestry road completed in 1935. This was much easier than floating the logs to Calgary via the Kananaskis and Bow rivers, as was done from a logging camp to the south that opened in 1886.

Kayaker on the Kananaskis River near Canoe Meadows.

The lower slopes of Mount Allan were mined for coal from 1947 to 1952. Today, one can see remnants of these developments along a hiking trail up Ribbon Creek.

At 8.5 kilometres past the Ribbon Creek area, a side-road climbs to the Fortress Mountain ski resort, which has survived several financial crises and ownership changes since it opened in 1969. The far slopes, leading steeply to a ridge overlooking Fortress Lake, are ablaze with wildflowers in early summer, if one doesn't mind walking alongside ski lifts. Just past the Fortress access road is the boundary to Peter Lougheed Provincial Park, which protects the finest mountain terrain in Kananaskis Country.

This trip ends at King Creek, just before the junction of Highway 40 with the Kananaskis Lakes Trail. It is well worth taking the level 800-metre walk up King Creek, shaded even in summer by its high walls. This narrow canyon was carved by glacial meltwaters, creating a passageway used today by bighorn sheep, elk and deer as they move from high meadows to a salt lick on the west side of the highway. Interpretive signs along the way explain the ancient forces of mountain building here as well as such things as lichens on the canyon walls.

Golden Eagle Migration

ROUTE: From the Canada Olympic Park traffic lights, drive 61 kilometres west on the Trans-Canada Highway and exit onto Highway 40; follow it south for 23 kilometres. At the Kananaskis Village turnoff, head west for 1 kilometre and turn right onto the Stoney Trail road, which in about 100 metres reaches a parking area. On foot, walk north of the vehicle barrier and turn right on the Hay Meadow trail. Follow it for less than a kilometre to a large clearing alongside the Kananaskis River (small buildings nearby).

DRIVING DISTANCE: About 85 kilometres one way.

NOTE: Canmore (95 kilometres west of Calgary on the Trans-Canada Highway) hosts the Golden Eagle Festival in mid-October during the fall migration. Phone (403) 678-1878 for information.

Scientist Peter Sherrington scans the skies above Patrick Peak in the Kananaskis Valley for migrating golden eagles.

It's hard to believe that less than an hour's drive west of Calgary, a major migration of birds with two-metre wingspans has been taking place for thousands of years—and no one knew about it. It wasn't until the early 1990s that ardent bird watcher Peter Sherrington discovered that 6,000 to 8,000 golden eagles were flying twice a year over the front ranges of the Rocky Mountains between wintering grounds as far south as Mexico and breeding areas in Alaska and the Yukon.

That discovery has since spawned a weekend-long Golden Eagle Festival in mid-October in Canmore. There, visitors can scan the skies through spotting scopes, talk to avid birders, perhaps see a trained eagle up close or take a guided hike up nearby Mount Lady Macdonald to view these magnificent birds riding thermal updrafts.

But if you want to see an average of 250 golden eagles in

one day, head to the Kananaskis Valley during the peak spring and fall migrations in March and October. Pack a good pair of binoculars (or, better yet, a spotting scope; you won't see these high flyers, other than as a tiny dot, with the naked eye), a picnic lunch, warm clothes and a folding chair. Perhaps the best viewing site is Hay Meadow, beside the tranquil Kananaskis River, with panoramic views of the valley and peaks such as Lorette, Allan, Bogart and Kidd. Your eyes, however, will mostly be trained east along the ridgeline of a peak, informally called Patrick, for the frequent passing of golden eagles.

The golden eagle is a majestic bird, with three times the visual acuity of humans. It is a fierce hunter, swooping down with powerful talons on snowshoe hares and, more rarely, young mountain goats or bighorn sheep. But an adult eagle doesn't usually eat during its long migration, which is a marvel of aerodynamics and energy efficiency.

Turning its wings 90 degrees into the wind, an eagle rises several hundred metres on an updraft, then glides on a descending angle of about one degree until it needs to climb again. Under good wind conditions, it can reach speeds of 120 kilometres per hour and probably cover up to 700 kilometres in a day. During the peak of the migration, eagles are often in the air from 8 a.m. to 8 p.m., resting at night above treeline or at an open expanse like the top of Plateau Mountain in southern Kananaskis Country.

Visitors to Hay Meadow can easily see several soaring golden eagles in a few minutes of spotting. But to get a true sense of this migration, be prepared to spend several hours in this magnificent spot. Consider that Sherrington and a handful of other unpaid volunteers have spent an average of 10 hours a day here seven months of the year for more than a decade, thus making a significant contribution to the understanding of these birds. By meticulously recording the passage of each eagle in the middle of this flyway, they can confirm, say, that breeding numbers are up in Alaska or that the mortality rate is high on southern wintering grounds, likely from hunters who prize their tail feathers.

Besides golden eagles, Sherrington and his fellow researchers have recorded some 225 bird species from Hay Meadow. Their sightings include many bald eagles; the occasional blue heron; large flocks of migrating ducks, geese and loons; the strange spectacle of normally stream-hugging dippers flying high at dusk; the rarely seen gyrfalcon and turkey vulture; and the first Alberta sighting of white-throated swifts. They've also seen plenty of deer, moose and elk, plus the odd bear, lynx and wolf. You, too, can see a lot of wildlife and the changing of the mountain seasons if, like Sherrington, you're willing to patiently sit and watch the natural world go by.

Kananaskis Country Loop

ROUTE: From Canada Olympic Park traffic lights, drive 61 kilometres west on the Trans-Canada Highway to the Kananaskis Country exit. Go 50 kilometres south on Highway 40 and turn right onto Kananaskis Lakes Trail, which provides access, in 12.5 kilometres, to Canadian Mount Everest Expedition Trail. The return trip follows the Smith-Dorrien/Spray Trail north for 60 kilometres to Canmore and then back to Calgary on the Trans-Canada Highway.
DRIVING DISTANCE: About 285 kilometres return.

The Kananaskis Country Loop is a driving tour of sharp contrasts through the impressive front ranges of the Rocky Mountains. The first half is smooth sailing south on immaculate pavement past the numerous recreational developments of Highway 40. The return trip north is down a gravel highway that offers mountain scenery unencumbered by tourist hordes.

There is some method to this madness. For good or ill, recreational developments in Kananaskis Country, such as ski hills, golf courses and hotels, have been concentrated along Highway 40 near Ribbon Creek. That leaves the Smith-Dorrien/Spray Valley in a fairly natural state, if you discount the Spray Lakes Reservoir, which preceded Kananaskis Country by nearly three decades. The creation of Spray Valley Provincial Park in 2000 prevents further development there. The area's jewel, at the southern end of this loop, lies within Peter Lougheed Provincial Park and is similarly protected.

This is primarily a driving tour that circumnavigates the Kananaskis Range via broad, parallel valleys. But there are plenty of opportunities to stop en route, along with a magnificent short hike to a hilltop overlooking the Kananaskis Lakes. For a detailed description of the attractions along Highway 40, see the Kananaskis Valley trip on pages 185-190.

Kananaskis Country is named for an Indian who, according to legend, made a miraculous recovery from an axe blow to the head. By contrast, Peter Lougheed, the former Conservative premier for whom the provincial park is named, survived a distinguished political career relatively unscathed. The provincial government created Kananaskis Country in 1977 as a 4000-square-kilometre mountain playground and a nearby alternative to the crowded mountain national parks. Unlike those parks, it was designated a multiple-use area that allowed some cattle grazing, logging and natural gas extraction to continue, especially on its eastern and southern reaches.

While the Ribbon Creek area was once logged and mined for coal, this central section of Kananaskis Country has primarily been devoted to recreational pursuits, most noticeably skiing, golfing, hiking and camping. There are also opportunities to fish, kayak, ride horses, cycle and even hunt for big game—at least outside Peter Lougheed Provincial Park.

Kananaskis Country also differs from the national parks in charging no entrance fees and allowing no towns. Nonetheless, hundreds of millions of dollars from oil royalties accumulated in the province's Heritage Fund were spent on roads and recreational facilities. Anyone who visits the 36-hole golf course, the RV park and campgrounds and even the deluxe visitor centres will agree the province went first class.

Still the main attraction, I hope, is the mountain environment. The peaks along Highway 40 are not only exquisite but also provide a graphic lesson in the forces of mountain building and erosion.

These mountains are made up of sediments deposited in inland seas several hundred million years ago and compressed into rocks such as limestones, dolomites and sandstones. Between 80 million and 40 million years ago, colliding tectonic plates deep below the earth's surface unleashed great forces from the west, causing these horizontal layers to be folded and fractured. Such folding is clearly evident in the south face of Mount Kidd. The fracturing created fault lines, along which older layers of rock were thrust up at a steep angle over younger rocks.

Today, the most visible layers in these peaks are the older, gray limestones, which overlay brown sandstones and shales. Limestone is particularly resistant to erosion and thus forms many of the impressive faces of the Opal Range, on the east side of Highway 40 across from Kananaskis Lakes.

These mountain ranges also influence the climate. The east side of the Kananaskis Valley is somewhat drier than the west, where the higher peaks of the Kananaskis Range attract more precipitation. I have often hiked in sunshine on the east while the western peaks were shrouded in clouds.

The Kananaskis Range, in turn, gets considerably less precipitation than the peaks along the Continental Divide on the west side of the Smith-Dorrien Highway, one valley to the west. The divide, which marks much of the Alberta-B.C. boundary, is the height of land separating river systems that flow to opposite sides of the continent.

At a T-junction 50 kilometres south of the Trans-Canada

Highway, turn right onto the Kanaskis Lakes Trail, which leads in 2 kilometres to the Smith-Dorrien/Spray Trail to the north. It is well worth detouring here to an interpretive trail that honours the first Canadian ascent of Mount Everest in 1982. To get there, continue on the Kananaskis Lakes Trail for another 10.5 kilometres to the White Spruce parking lot and the start of the trail.

This is a splendid 2.4-kilometre loop trail that climbs through a thick forest of spruce, pine and Douglas fir to a high lookout between the Upper and Lower Kananaskis lakes. The impressive view over an upper lake ringed with glacier-capped mountains was apparently even more spectacular before an earthen dam was built in the 1950s, drowning several forested islands and enlarging the lake.

The return drive along the Kananaskis Trail passes Boulton Creek, where archaeological digs have uncovered stone flakes and spear points used by aboriginal peoples more than 8,000 years ago. Farther on, nestled in the lodgepole pine forest, is the Peter Lougheed Provincial Park visitor centre, which features a number of hands-on interpretive displays.

The Smith-Dorrien/Spray Trail crosses the muted Kananaskis River and swings past the Lower Kananaskis Lake on pavement that soon gives way to good gravel. In 1841, James Sinclair led a group of 200 Metis from Manitoba through this valley and over the nearby White Man Pass en route to a settlement in Oregon, which the British hoped to claim.

A number of peaks along this valley—including Indefatigable, Invincible, Black Prince, Chester and Sparrowhawk—are named after cruisers and destroyers involved, often disastrously, in the Battle of Jutland during World War I. Other mountains, on the left, honour commanding officers from the same war.

Past the Black Prince parking lot and hidden by a line of mountains to the west are the sizable Haig and Robertson glaciers. Farther on at Mud Lake are trails leading to Burstall Pass and Chester Lake, two of the more popular hiking and cross-country ski destinations in Kananaskis Country. The small earthen dam at Mud Lake marks a height of land from which creeks flow both north and south.

Just beyond the boundary to Peter Lougheed Provincial Park, you can pull in to Engadine Lodge for afternoon tea and pastries and enjoy fine views across the meadows to Mount Smuts and Commonwealth Peak.

Back on the road, the lengthy Spray Lakes Reservoir soon comes into view. The construction of Canyon Dam here in 1949 flooded smaller lakes and diverted much of the Spray River's flow from Banff to Canmore. The lake levels fluctuate significantly to meet electrical demands, preventing plants from growing along the shoreline. Once-plentiful native cut-throat have largely disappeared from the lake, replaced by stocked lake trout and whitefish that attract many anglers, particularly those who fish through the ice in winter.

Beyond the reservoir, the road narrows markedly and follows a winding course to White Man's Gap. A small pull-off provides a commanding view over the expanding town of Canmore and the surrounding Bow Corridor. This lofty perch is at the lip of a hanging valley, left dangling high above the Bow Valley after the latter was carved by advancing glaciers. The descent is continuously steep to Canmore, requiring steady braking.

Fall Larch Hike

ROUTE: From the Canada Olympic Park traffic lights, drive 61 kilometres west on the Trans-Canada Highway and then 68 kilometres south on Highway 40 to the Highwood Pass parking lot.
DRIVING DISTANCE: 129 kilometres one way.
NOTE: The moderate hike into the upper headwaters of Pocaterra Creek rises about 100 metres over 2 kilometres.

Alberta lacks the fiery blaze of red and orange maples that marks the coming of fall in eastern Canada. Yet our southern mountains are blessed with the unique spectacle of a conifer that loses its needles each fall. In late September, an annual pilgrimage begins to see stands of alpine larch briefly turning a stunning yellowy-orange before shedding their needles. The short hike into upper Pocaterra Creek in the heart of Kananaskis Country is a lovely way for visitors of all ages to witness this rite of fall.

But don't expect solitude. Like the overrun Larch Valley near Lake Louise, the late September walk into Pocaterra Valley is rapidly gaining popularity, especially on sunny weekends, when young children and even small dogs join the hordes. The reason is easy access. Alpine larches grow near treeline, generally at an elevation around 2,200 metres, meaning a fair climb on foot is usually needed to reach them. But thanks to the highest highway in Canada, visitors can see larch from the car as they reach Highwood Pass.

The finest larch stands in this area, however, are about a 45-minute walk away in a stunning alpine valley. From the parking lot, the route follows the Highwood Meadows interpretive trail for about 100 metres before angling left on a dirt trail through a small grassy draw marked by a large depression. A well-beaten trail ascends left through often muddy woods and over a treed ridge. Emerging onto an avalanche slope, hikers can pause to look north along Pocaterra Creek to the jagged Elpoca Mountain on the horizon. The trail continues over a rock slide, then follows a small stream to a tiny pond ringed by larch. Ambitious hikers can continue farther up the valley, turning left for Grizzly Col or right for Little Highwood Pass, though both involve much steeper climbs that soon leave the larch behind. Speaking of grizzlies, these bears often dig winter dens in larch stands in the Canadian Rockies.

Alpine larch are also commonly known as subalpine larch

or as Lyall's larch, the latter for Scottish naturalist David Lyall, who first described these trees in 1858. They appear high in the mountains of the Pacific Northwest, southeast B.C. and the U.S. and Canadian Rockies. Within the latter, they are found as far north as Clearwater Pass, east of Bow Summit, beyond which the climate is apparently too cool to support them.

Alpine larch typically grow on moist, north-facing slopes near treeline, where their only competition is subalpine fir and Engelmann spruce, which tend to be more stunted at this elevation. Larch are intolerant of shade, needing considerable light to develop their soft, translucent green needles each spring and summer. Occasionally, larch will invade areas considered to be above treeline, such as the alpine meadows

Hikers passing a stand of alpine larch in the upper Pocaterra Valley.

around Healy Pass in Banff National Park. In parts of Banff's Bow Valley where fire has created sufficient openings (such as near Castle Junction), larch can be found as low as 1,900 metres. With their thin bark, alpine larch are themselves susceptible to fire, though major burns are uncommon near tree-line.

The alpine larch survives up here because of its hardiness—its ability to withstand cool summers and cold winters, high winds, avalanches and snow patches that linger into July. But it's a tenuous existence. Larch don't germinate well at this elevation, and survivors grow very slowly during their first two decades; in one study, 10-year-old seedlings were only 4 centimetres high. During this time, however, they develop strong tap and lateral roots in the rocky soils. The annual loss of their needles also helps them withstand winter dehydration.

Once well established, alpine larch can live for centuries, with the older trees generally found at higher elevations. A dead, 838-year-old larch was found in Waterton Lakes National Park and a living 735-year-old specimen was discovered near Storm Mountain in Banff National Park. In Manning Provincial Park in southwest B.C., several alpine larch are believed to be nearly 2,000 years old, which would make them Canada's oldest trees. Alpine larch are rarely uprooted, though their knobby black limbs and trunk, weakened by heart rot, may be toppled by high winds.

In well-sheltered, healthy stands like those at Panorama Ridge, above Taylor Lake in Banff National Park, larch can grow to 20 metres high. They are also seen in profusion in Banff's Bow Valley, along Highway 93 south of Castle Junction and in many parts of Kananaskis Country, especially at Little Elbow Pass. To find your own secluded larch grove, gaze up to treeline as you're driving through Banff or Kananaskis in the fall and watch for dense patches of yellow.

Yamnuska

ROUTE: From the Canada Olympic Park traffic lights, drive 65 kilometres west on the Trans-Canada Highway, take the Seebe/Exshaw exit and go 4 kilometres north on Highway 1X. Head 2.2 kilometres east on Highway 1A and turn left on a gravel road that soon leads to a parking lot.

DRIVING DISTANCE: About 71 kilometres one way.

NOTE: The trail to Yamnuska's east ridge climbs 430 metres in elevation over 3.5 kilometres. Hikers should be in reasonably good physical condition and equipped with sturdy boots.

With its impressive face of gray limestone, Yamnuska is a landmark peak guarding the entrance to the Rocky Mountains west of Calgary. It also overlooks an incredibly rich mixture of natural features and wildlife habitats, befitting a designated natural area. From late spring through fall, it is an excellent choice for a short, though steep, hike to its east ridge, with superb views over the Bow Valley.

The peak is officially known as Mount John Laurie, in honour of the man who devoted much of his life to helping Alberta's aboriginal people. But most locals know it as Yamnuska, a Stoney term meaning either "wall of stone" or "flat mountain." It is affectionately called Yam by climbers, who have put more than 70 routes up its south face, making it the most important rock wall in the Canadian Rockies.

Yamnuska marks the transition from foothills to Rocky Mountain front ranges. As well, it often marks a rather abrupt change from cloudy mountain weather to clear eastern skies. On such days, the peak is often framed by striking bands of arching white clouds.

The base of Yamnuska's south face also clearly delineates a famous geological dividing line known as the McConnell Thrust Fault. Here, 525-million-year-old Eldon Formation limestone rocks have been thrust some 40 kilometres east, up

The limestone south face of Yamnuska.

and over top of 75-million-year-old mudstones and sand-stones, disturbing the softer underlying rocks very little in the process. The McConnell Thrust—named for geologist R.G. McConnell, who helped map the area's rocks for the Geological Survey of Canada in the 1880s—is one of the world's major faults, extending some 400 kilometres. Along the fault line near Yamnuska, calcareous springs reach the sur-face and help feed a surprising number of small lakes and ponds.

Yamnuska's lower slopes and valley bottom are also a nat-uralist's delight, reflecting the merging here of mountain, foothills and prairie ecosystems. More than 180 bird species have been recorded in the area, ranging from great gray and horned owls to ospreys and northern orioles. Wildflowers are abundant (more than 300 species identified), highlighted by brilliant spring displays of prairie crocus and yellow lady's slippers. The Yamnuska area is similarly rich in human history, with findings of prehistoric tipi rings, hearths and stone tools.

More recent human usage, however, threatened to significantly impact Yamnuska's unique natural heritage. A sandstone quarry has long been in operation at the mountain's base, and random camping and off-road vehicle use were steadily increasing, as were the number of trails crisscrossing the lower mountain slopes. A plan for a recreational vehicle park below Yamnuska was the final impetus for the Alberta government to, in 1997, create Yamnuska Natural Area, covering 1,600 hectares below John Laurie and Goat mountains.

To minimize visitor impacts, a new parking area was created at the east entrance of the natural area and random camping and off-road vehicle use was eliminated. With the help of volunteers and some minimum-security prisoners, a single access trail was built to the base of the climbing cliffs, avoiding the quarry, which continues to be mined but within its current boundaries. Recently, the government announced plans to add the Yamnuska Natural Area to the Bow Valley Wildland Park, thus providing more enforcement teeth for protecting the area.

From the parking lot, the trail to Yamnuska's east ridge climbs steadily through a lovely aspen forest to a junction. Straight ahead lies the climbers' access route, which switchbacks steeply up towards the east end of the south face. Instead, head right on the gentler hiking trail, which traverses east before ascending more steeply alongside a small, steep-sided valley, which even in late summer contains a trickle of water. Notice the lush growth of tall spruce and aspen in the shaded valley and compare it to the stunted aspen and grasses of the exposed slope to the right. The thick forest soon gives way to more barren slopes with scattered trees and outcrops of shale.

In about 45 minutes, hikers reach a bench providing magnificent views over the Bow Valley, which is several kilometres wide here. To the southeast is the old glacial lakebed of Morley Flats and, beyond, the entrance to Kananaskis Valley. Farther west, three of the four peaks of Mount Lougheed are visible, as is the summit of Mount Sparrowhawk. Below and to the east, Nakoda Lodge can be spotted on the edge of Chief Hector Lake. Those with sufficient energy can climb another 130 vertical metres to the ridge crest (offering views into the next valley) and perhaps continue up to the east end of Yamnuska's main wall. A somewhat down-sloping trail traverses west under impressive vertical walls of yellow and gray limestone but is exposed to scree slopes below and rockfall hazard from climbers above. The safest choice is to return the way you came up.

Heart Creek

ROUTE: From the Canada Olympic Park traffic lights, drive 74 kilometres west on the Trans-Canada Highway. Take the Heart Creek/Lac Des Arcs exit and go south on the overpass to reach the parking lot and trailhead.
NOTE: Hiking distance is 3 kilometres one way. Allow at least two hours.

This is a pleasant family stroll up the narrow and biologically diverse Heart Creek Valley. The trail is mainly flat, criss-crossing the creek seven times on wooden bridges. Visitors armed with interpretive brochures can learn about the creek ecology while young children can float sticks and, despite parental warnings, hop on streamside rocks. For the intrepid, there's the option of a strenuous hike and scramble to the top of Heart Mountain.

From the parking lot, the trail initially parallels the highway as it crosses over a treed hump. Turn right at a junction (700 metres) to enter Heart Creek Valley, a defile between

Crossing Heart Creek.

Mount McGillivray on the right and Heart Mountain on the left. Soon the gurgling waters and high walls swallow the highway's din.

Unlike the broad, glacially sculpted Bow Valley behind you, this narrow, V-shaped valley was formed over thousands of years by Heart Creek. Although tiny today, the spring-fed creek was undoubtedly a torrent at the end of the last ice age, as melting waters hastened the process of carving a channel through the softer layers of sedimentary rock.

The tall cliffs shield the valley from the full brunt of warm chinook winds that lash the Bow Valley in winter, often drying and damaging trees. As a result, Heart Creek has a cooler but more consistent climate that allows a diversity of plants to thrive. Mixed in with the usual low mountain aspen, pine, spruce and occasional Douglas fir are paper birch and even some shrubby Douglas maple.

The rock walls lengthen into high cliffs halfway up the short valley. Large slabs of rock thrusting almost vertically upward along fault lines are clearly visible on the lower slopes of Heart Mountain, to the left. Look high on the right for small caves, scooped from the limestone walls by the forces of water, ice and wind. On lower rocks, small spruce have anchored their roots in cracks formed by long cycles of freezing and thawing.

What the mountains give, they also take away. A number of trees have been all but bowled over in one place, apparently by a slide from the slopes above.

The trail ends at an abrupt narrowing of the valley, where the creek spills in a small waterfall over a rock step. At low water, it is possible to edge around a tight, slippery corner to get a close look at the falls. In winter, climbers frequent this tongue of frozen water to practice their ice technique.

Heart Mountain Option

Accomplished hikers who don't mind a short piece of climbing can ascend the northwest ridge of Heart Mountain. It is named for the heart shape of its upper reaches, best seen from the 1A Highway to the north. The distinctive formation is the result of a prominent downward fold, called a syncline, in the rock strata.

Be forewarned: the rocky ascent to the first summit is relentlessly steep, gaining nearly 900 metres of elevation in less than 3 kilometres. Sturdy hiking boots are recommended, especially for the descent. At one point, it's necessary to climb about 5 metres of rock on good holds to gain the upper ridge, to the left. Most other difficulties can be avoided by detouring left. If in doubt along the way, turn around and enjoy your lofty vantage point before descending.

The rewards of reaching the top are splendid views of the Bow Valley and peaks to the south. Those seeking further adventure can carry on to the true summit and descend on another northwest ridge to the east to make a complete circuit. The rest of the trip is considerably easier than the ascent but is a full day's outing. For detailed route instructions, consult *Kananaskis Country Trail Guide*, by Gillean Daffern.

1A Highway Tour

ROUTE: From the junction of Crowchild Trail and Nose Hill Drive N.W., follow the 1A Highway northwest through Cochrane and Exshaw to the Trans-Canada Highway overpass just east of Canmore.

DRIVING DISTANCE: 94 kilometres one way.

For many years, the 1A Highway was the major transportation corridor between Calgary and Banff. Indeed, parts of this route along the north side of the Bow River date back more than a century. Today, the 1A Highway provides a leisurely alternative approach to the mountains as it winds along the north side of the Bow River. The unhurried pace also encourages travellers to pull over at the many points of historical and natural interest along the way.

The trip initially traverses a high plateau overlooking a succession of plains, foothills and mountains. James Hector, a member of the Palliser Expedition, travelled this way in 1858 and remarked upon the profusion of flowers and exhilarating view of distant, snowy peaks. On the right, the rolling hills that house the acreages of Bearspaw are excellent examples of knob and kettle topography, formed at the end of the last ice age by stagnating glaciers.

In 1875, Reverend John McDougall rode east along this route from his mission at Morleyville to visit the new North-West Mounted Police post at Fort Calgary. Known as the Morleyville Trail, this rutted track became an important link between the two settlements.

The plateau ends suddenly on the brow of Cochrane Hill,

McDougall Memorial United Church and the grave of Methodist missionary George McDougall, who died in 1876.

offering a stunning view of Cochrane, the Bow Valley and the Rocky Mountain front ranges. The aforementioned Hector, who spent a night camped below, called this magical spot Dream Hill. The winding highway that once descended the long, steep incline was replaced in the late 1940s by a more direct plunge. A sharp turn at the bottom, resulting in numerous backyard crashes, was eliminated a decade later when the road was rerouted behind the town.

Cochrane is named for Senator Matthew Cochrane, who, in 1881, established western Canada's first big ranch, a 40,000-hectare spread based just west of the current town. The Cochrane Ranche briefly increased traffic along the Morleyville Trail. But harsh winters and poor management decimated the cattle herd, prompting Cochrane to move much of the operation south to near Waterton in 1883.

The construction of the Canadian Pacific Railway through the Bow Valley in 1883 drained the route of most traffic until the arrival of the automobile two decades later. William Cochrane (no relation to the town) made the first recorded car trip through here, driving his vehicle perhaps as far as Morley. In 1909, Norman Lougheed made the first complete car trip from Calgary to Banff, a full day's excursion. Though several bridges and culverts had been added a year earlier, much of the route followed wagon ruts.

The road was gravelled in 1924-25, making motor travel much easier, at least when the surface was dry. It was now called the Blue Trail, its blue signposts corresponding with colour-coded maps published by Alberta's motor clubs. The road was paved in 1932 and renamed Highway 2, later changed to Highway 1. Rebuilt in 1947, the route number was again changed, to the current 1A, a decade later when the new Highway 1, the Trans-Canada, opened south of the Bow River.

West of Cochrane, the highway soon passes Ghost Lake. The lake was formed in 1929 when Calgary Power built a hydroelectric dam on the Bow River. Ghost Lake is now a popular spot for sailing, wind surfing and ice sailing, thanks to the strong winds that funnel through the Bow Valley.

Beyond Ghost Lake, the road traverses an open bench above the river. Soon visible on the left is the historic McDougall Memorial United Church. Here, George McDougall and his son John established Morleyville, a Methodist mission among the Stoney Indians, in 1873. It was one of southern Alberta's early settlements other than fur-trading and whisky forts. In 1876, George McDougall died and was buried in the church yard after losing his way on the winter prairie to the east.

The Stoney were a Sioux tribe apparently pushed west in the early 1700s to the foothills and mountains of south-central Alberta. Their normal route west veered north of the current highway from Morley and followed the Ghost River to Devil's Lake (now Minnewanka) and past today's Banff. In the mid-1800s, missionaries and explorers followed this route into the mountains.

After signing Treaty No. 7 in 1877, the Stoney were moved onto their current reserve. Frustrated by what they saw as restrictive hunting and travel regulations, a breakaway group moved north in the mid-1890s to sacred ancestral grounds at Kootenay Plains, near Saskatchewan River Crossing. With the bison and other game animals largely decimated, the Stoney turned to farming. But their greatest resource has been the abundant supplies of natural gas under the reserve.

At Stoney Indian Park, 12 kilometres west of Morley, the Stoney maintain a small herd of bison on grasslands above the Bow River. Here, where Old Fort Creek enters the river canyon, the Hudson's Bay Company in 1832 established Peigan Post, a short-lived trading post burned to the ground by Blood Indians soon after it was abandoned.

The Stoney are also venturing into tourism. The nearby Nakoda Lodge, built in 1981, is a handsome conference facility and guest lodge on the shores of Chief Hector Lake. The conference facility contains a learning centre, a small museum and a gallery dedicated to native art. Many people come to Nakoda Lodge for Sunday brunch and to admire the view across the lake to Mount John Laurie, commonly known as Yamnuska (see pages 201-204).

Running along the base of Yamnuska's high cliffs is the McConnell Thrust, which separates the foothills here from the front range mountains. The fault marks the line along which a massive block of older limestone thrust up over a much younger layer of shale. The resistant limestone now forms Yamnuska's vertical grey cliffs, prized among rock climbers, while the shale has largely been eroded into the scree slopes below.

Near the town of Exshaw, the process of erosion has been aided by mining. Here, limestone is processed into cement and related products at two plants. A third plant processes magnesite, mined elsewhere into magnesium oxide. From 1902 to 1930, the eastern park entrance to Banff National Park was at Exshaw. The boundary was then retracted to its current position to allow for commercial developments in the Canmore area.

Just beyond Exshaw is the Grotto Canyon parking lot, where visitors can take a fine 2.5-kilometre interpretive walk. The canyon was primarily carved over a few thousand years by the rush of glacial meltwaters. Today, the stream bed is nearly dry, allowing visitors to walk along the narrow canyon bottom for much of its length. High walls shelter the canyon, allowing unusual vegetation such as Douglas maple to grow here. Near the end of this hike, the canyon forks. A right branch climbs quickly to a small waterfall, while the left leads to a broader valley.

Grotto Canyon has long been a sacred place for aboriginal people who painted red figures on smooth panels of rock. These centuries-old paintings, called pictographs, are extremely fragile, so admire any you see at a distance. Climbers are also attracted to these short, steep walls. They have drilled bolts, fairly permanent pieces of shiny protection, into the rock to safeguard first and subsequent ascents.

Back in the car, motorists soon pass Gap Lake, a popular fishing spot for brown trout and mountain whitefish up to 2 kilograms in size. In 1800, explorer and mapmaker David Thompson became the first white person to enter this part of the Bow Valley, when he led a party on foot as far west as Gap Lake. The ascending road beyond the lake is a good place to see bighorn sheep and to view the four summits of Mount Lougheed across the valley.

Not far from Canmore's outskirts is the Old Camp picnic area, site of a government relief camp during the 1930s. The

Depression project gave work to about 80 men, who maintained and upgraded the 1A Highway for 20 cents a day plus room and board, clothing and a tobacco ration.

Canmore Historical Tour

ROUTE: From the Canada Olympic Park traffic lights, drive 89 kilometres west on the Trans-Canada Highway. Take the first Canmore exit onto Highway 1A west, turning left at the traffic lights and left onto 8 Street and into downtown Canmore. To reach the Canmore Nordic Centre, turn left at the west end of 8 Street and follow the signs for 4 kilometres.

DRIVING DISTANCE: About 95 kilometres one way.

NOTE: The Canmore Museum and Geoscience Centre is open daily 9:00 a.m. to 5:00 p.m. Phone (403) 678-2462. For information on summer and winter activities at the Canmore Nordic Centre, phone (403) 678-2400.

In recent years, Canmore has become a modern boom town, attracting upscale tourism and residents seeking a mountain address. But the town was built on the booms and busts of a much sootier resource—coal. This trip is an excursion into that past, plus a brief introduction to Canmore's newer attractions.

Canmore, from a Gaelic word meaning "big head," originated in 1883 as a scattering of businesses that served the construction of the national railway as it moved west into the mountains. The new railway brought to Canmore a Canadian Pacific Railway divisional point and prospectors seeking coal to fuel the train engines.

In 1886, the Canmore Coal Company began tapping the rich coal seams beneath the mountains south of town. Soon, other coal mining communities—with names like Prospect, Georgetown, Mineside, Anthracite and Bankhead—sprang up between Canmore and Banff. Most of these instant towns were short-lived, quickly becoming ghost towns.

To visit the grassy site of one of these former mining towns, drive up to the Canmore Nordic Centre, which sits on reclaimed coal mining lands. The Nordic Centre was developed to host the cross-country skiing and biathlon events at the 1988 Winter Olympic Games. Today, its maze of trails attracts competitive and recreational skiers in winter and hikers and mountain bikers in summer. Mountain bikes and cross-country skis can be rented at the site.

The Georgetown interpretive loop is a pleasant forest walk, reached by following the signs from behind the biathlon range (a "Summer Trails" brochure, showing all the Nordic Centre trails, can be picked up at the day lodge). The trail descends through a mixed forest of pine, white spruce and aspen, typical of the lower vegetation belt on mountains, known as montane. This bench above Canmore is sufficiently high and sheltered to retain much of the precipitation that falls on this dry east side of the mountains. Still, snow-making equipment is needed on some ski trails to make up for nature's shortcomings, though a strong chinook wind can quickly melt any type of snow.

The trail leads to a clearing once occupied by Georgetown, a vibrant coal-mining community of Italians, Poles and Germans. Although it contained fewer than 200 residents, Georgetown boasted cottages with electricity and running water, a company store and a community hall where a local orchestra frequently played.

Yet Georgetown only survived from 1912 to 1915. It fell victim to falling coal prices and a lack of financing at the outbreak of World War I. When the mine closed, many of the buildings were skidded on logs down to Canmore, where some are still in use. Today, all that remains of Georgetown are the footings of these vanished buildings in a grassy clearing.

The road back into town passes Mineside, now a neighbourhood of west Canmore that contains the houses of many former miners. Above the Bow River nearby are several stately houses, dating back to the 1890s, that were built for mine officials. Mining continued above Mineside until 1979, when the last of Canmore's coal mines closed.

While residential and commercial development is now rampant throughout an expanding Canmore, there are still vivid examples of its early days. Heading back east along 8th Street (Main Street), visitors can drop into the Canmore Hotel, built in 1890. Across the avenue from the hotel is the Canmore Museum and Geoscience Centre, which houses mining memorabilia and a doll collection.

Farther east is the Ralph Connor Memorial United Church, in operation since it was built in 1890. Its first minister, Charles Gordon, was responsible for a district that encompassed towns, railway stations and mining and lumber camps reaching to Field, B.C. Gordon later received international acclaim under his pen name, Ralph Connor, for novels such as *Black Rock* and *Sky Pilot*.

Nearby, on the banks of Policeman's Creek, is the town's original North-West Mounted Police barracks. This mud-chinked log structure was erected in 1892 in response to complaints about an increasingly rowdy group of single men, employed by the railway and mines, who constituted the bulk of the town's 500 citizens. Vacated by the police force in 1929, the barracks became a private residence for 40 years. It is now a provincial historic site that is being restored by the Centennial Museum Society of Canmore.

Just east of the barracks, you can finish the Canmore tour by taking a short stroll on the boardwalk that passes through marshy grasses near Policeman's Creek. The creek, controlled by an upstream sluice gate, is one of the braided channels of the Bow River that meander through central Canmore. The town's streams and backwaters, some fed by springs, provide important spawning habitat for trout and winter refuge for hundreds of mallard ducks.

Grassi Lakes

ROUTE: Follow the directions for the Canmore Historical Tour (pages 212-214) to the Canmore Nordic Centre turnoff. Continue on Spray Lakes Road for another kilometre, turning left on a short access road to reach Grassi Lakes parking lot and trailhead.

NOTE: Hiking distance is 2 kilometres one way, 250 metres elevation gain. Allow two hours or more return.

Grassi Lakes is one of the better short walks in the Canadian Rockies and a fine family outing. It offers expansive views of the Bow Valley and, at trail's end, two exquisite ponds backed by a high rock wall. Long a spiritual place for natives, Grassi Lakes is today a tranquil retreat less than an hour from the bustle of Canmore.

Once called Twin Lakes, these blue-green ponds were renamed in honour of Lawrence Grassi, an Italian woodcutter

Author at Grassi Lakes. Photo by Teresa Michalak.

who came to Canmore in 1916 to work in the underground coal mines. Here, he and fellow miners took advantage of a strike in the 1920s to build the stone steps, bridges and strategically placed benches on this well-graded trail. Many of these features have subsequently been replaced. An accomplished climber, Grassi is also known for the meticulous and sensitive trails he built around Lake O'Hara in Yoho National Park.

From the parking lot, the trail leads up through a mature forest of pine broken by aspen and underlain by low shrubs, early-season violets, Indian paintbrush and wild strawberries. Higher, a scattering of moisture-loving birch foreshadows the emergence of a series of tiny streams seeping across the trail. Farther along, water and vegetation continue a fascinating interplay, evident in mosses growing from dripping rocks and algae waving from their underwater anchors.

The trail swings into a hillside clearing that overlooks the reservoir and town of Canmore and provides views across the valley to the peaks of the Fairholme Range. Though the Bow Valley here is but 2 kilometres wide, it has been crammed over the years with human developments. Visible are two highways, a railway, coal-mining scars and, most recently, housing and tourism complexes spreading up both sides of the valley.

Close at hand is a shiny steel penstock, which funnels dammed water from the hanging valley above to the reservoir below. It is part of the Spray Hydro System, in operation since 1951 and capable of meeting the electrical needs of 100,000 people. Aesthetically more pleasing is a large waterfall splashing down the rock face. In winter, it freezes into a swath of ice that attracts many climbers.

The trail climbs more steeply up rock steps, complete with a handrail, and then levels out as it crosses a rushing stream emptying out of the first lake. The blue-green waters here are replaced by a deeper blue in the upper lake.

Despite the visual presence of nearby power lines and penstocks, this place still conveys the magical sense that it must have held for natives who used this valley for 11,000 years. They carved their stories in the rocks and sought shelter in caves above the upper lake. The honeycombed cliffs are the 400-million-year-old remnants of a reef that developed in a shallow sea.

In the mid-1800s, the passage above these cliffs between Ha Ling Peak and Mount Rundle became a favoured access route for crossing the mountains into present-day British Columbia. One of the most remarkable treks through this White Man's Gap was undertaken by James Sinclair, who led 200 Metis settlers from Manitoba through the mountains to Oregon in 1841.

Return to the parking lot via an old fire road, which passes the remnants of a log cabin in the woods along the way.

Calgary to Banff

ROUTE: From the traffic lights at Canada Olympic Park, drive 110 kilometres west on the Trans-Canada Highway to the eastern entrance to Banff.

Think of the Trans-Canada Highway west of Calgary not as four lanes of high-speed freeway between points A and B but as a means of being transported through a fascinating corridor of natural and human history. On aesthetic grounds alone, this is one of the finest entrances to a mountain range imaginable. Even frequent visitors to the mountains can admire vistas that change with the seasons, the weather and subtle variations in lighting.

This route between Calgary and Banff was accidentally forged by a group of Irish-American gold seekers in 1864-65. Leaving the Banff area for the North Saskatchewan River to the north, they got lost and ended up following the Bow River to present-day Calgary.

For many years, the road west of Calgary followed the 1A

Highway, now a quiet backwater on the north side of the Bow River (see the 1A Highway Tour on pages 207-212 for a complete description). Today's Trans-Canada Highway was built on the river's south side in the late 1950s and was upgraded to a four-lane freeway a decade later.

The initial stretch of highway bisects rolling farmlands, where herds of cattle can often be spotted. The strong chinook winds that sweep the Bow Valley keep these fields clear of snow most of the winter, allowing cattle, deer and even some non-migrating ducks to feed.

About 15 kilometres west of Canada Olympic Park, the highway climbs to a hilltop offering a panoramic view over plains, forested foothills and the Rocky Mountains. Among the more prominent front range peaks are Mount Glasgow and Banded Peak, to the southwest, which often retain their snow cover well into the summer.

The road soon dips to cross Jumpingpound Creek. Along the creek to the north is a cliff, over which aboriginal people used to drive buffalo to their death, hence the name. The leisurely curious can take a pleasant detour here by following a gravel road north and west through the countryside, rejoining the Trans-Canada at the Sibbald Creek Trail exit.

Not far beyond, the road crosses the first of several low, parallel ridges that mark the start of the foothills. The ridges are generally underlain by resistant sandstones, while the dips in between are of softer shale. Where the sandstone is exposed, the ridges are called hogbacks. The underlying bedrock in these foothills is a complex structure of thrust faults and folds, created by the same great forces that forged the mountains to the west.

In depressions along the highway are small, reedy sloughs, which provide important habitat for nesting and migratory birds. A pothole slough beside the Sibbald Creek Trail exit is often the best place in the Calgary area to see migrating trumpeter swans in the spring.

The road climbs to its highest point at Scott Lake Hill, where the elevation and sheltered slopes allow thick coniferous forests to grow. The views on the descent are superb, as the bending road unveils a continuously expanding sweep of peaks.

The ensuing stretch of the Morley Flats is largely barren and windswept. Its underground formations nonetheless harbour large quantities of natural gas, enriching the coffers of the Stoney, whose reserve is situated here. The flats east of the Morley interchange feature impressive examples of drumlins. These are tapered hills of till or gravel shaped by glaciers that flowed eastward over them, leaving the blunt nose facing upstream and the pointed tail downstream.

During the last ice age, glaciers advancing east from the Lake Louise area carved the U-shaped valley that is clearly visible along the Bow Corridor. An arm of this glacier blocked the Kananaskis Valley, creating a glacial lake fed by meltwaters from mountain glaciers to the south. The lake drained when the glaciers disappeared some 10,000 years ago, leaving behind this flat valley bottom. The glaciers also deposited in the Bow Valley large quantities of unsorted material known as till. The sand and gravel deposits near Bow Valley Provincial Park, for example, are more than 80 metres deep.

To the north of the park is the impressive face of Yamnuska (officially known as Mount John Laurie), a popular rock-climbing spot. The McConnell Thrust at the base of Yamnuska's face marks the geological boundary between foothills and the mountain front ranges. The abrupt change in elevation here is largely due to the limestone mountain faces, which are much more resistant to erosion than the softer shales and sandstones of the foothills.

The highway soon takes a sweeping bend around Lac Des Arcs, a shallow lake fed by the Bow River. In spring and fall, a diversity of ducks, geese and swans stop here during their migration and can be observed from a new lakeshore interpretive trail. The fierce winds that buffet the lake also attract summer wind-surfers and winter ice-boaters.

William Van Horne, the president of the Canadian Pacific Railway, wanted to build a resort along Lac Des Arcs after passing through the area in the late nineteenth century. Those plans were quickly scuttled when a subsequent visit revealed a much lower, muddier lake.

The area has, however, long attracted development, as the cement plant across the lake indicates. Indeed, limestone rock from Exshaw Mountain has been feeding plants here since 1906. At the nearby Grotto Mountain, which harbours an extensive network of caves, lime was first commercially extracted in 1884 by a man named McCanleish. After he mysteriously disappeared on a trip to Calgary, an employee, Edwin Loder, assumed the operation.

A more vivid incident is commemorated at Dead Man's Flats. Here, in 1904, a French immigrant farmer, Jean Marret, was killed by his axe-wielding brother, Francois, who had complained of strange noises in his head. Found guilty and insane, Francois was dispatched to an asylum in Ponoka, south of Edmonton.

The boundaries of Canmore now stretch east to Dead Man's Flats and encompass a steadily increasing amount of tourism and housing development in this narrow valley. For the first three decades of this century, this area was located within Rocky Mountains National Park. The boundaries of the park, renamed Banff National Park, were retracted westward in 1930 to allow for development in the Canmore area.

Beyond Canmore, motorists are accompanied into Banff by the long flank of Mount Rundle. It is actually a massif, or a series of individual peaks. The northeast face displays high cliffs of limestone and dolomite at the base and summit and scree slopes of shale in between. The mountain is named after Robert Rundle, a Methodist missionary who travelled among the area's native tribes in the 1840s. Straight ahead is the impressively folded Cascade Mountain, named for the waterfall that splits its face and attracts winter ice-climbers.

A road from Calgary reached the Banff park gates in 1906, but automobiles were officially banned from the park until 1915. Once the gates opened, there was no turning back. Today, several million people pass through the gates by car every year. Just before Banff townsite, the road passes the Cascade Power Plant, its hydroelectric generator fed by waters from Lake Minnewanka. Across the highway from the power plant is the grassy site of Anthracite, a coal-mining town that existed from 1886 to 1904.

Banff

There is more to the town of Banff and its environs than the Banff Springs Hotel and a strip of high-priced shopping malls. A block or two removed from Banff Avenue, the din of cars and cash registers is replaced by the quiet and beauty of a small mountain town. From the centre of Banff, those on foot can embark on lovely walks along the Bow River or amble around the spring-fed marshes below the historic Cave and Basin. Motorists can tour along Tunnel Mountain Drive or head to Lake Minnewanka, both of which offer ample viewpoints and opportunities for short walks. The three trips described below are just a sampling of Banff's natural and historic delights, which may surprise even frequent and/or jaded visitors to Alberta's most famous town.

Banff Historical Tour

Route: From the south side of the Bow River bridge in Banff, drive 1.3 kilometres west to the Cave and Basin parking lot. The Banff Park Museum is located on the north side of the bridge.

NOTE: For hours and admission prices, phone Cave and Basin at (403) 762-1566 and Banff Park Museum at (403) 762-1558.

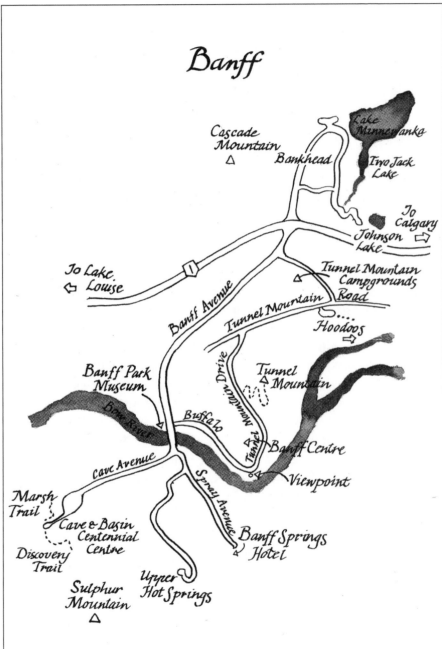

Cave and Basin

The cradle of Canada's national park system is a steamy hole in the ground with an acrid stench. In 1883, William McCardell shimmied through the hole and down a crude ladder into a cavern filled with hot sulphurous waters. McCardell and his two companions, railway surveyors in search of gold, laid claim to these hot pools. But it was a federal government eager to promote tourism that in 1885 set aside 26 square kilometres of land, later expanded to become Canada's first national park.

Log bath-houses were soon erected, attracting tourists and those seeking cures for everything from syphilis to gunshot wounds. For a time, the mineral waters were bottled and sold as an aid to digestion, the liver and the kidneys. By the 1920s, the Cave and Basin was a comfortable spa with a swimming pool.

Today, tired tourists revive themselves not at these bath-houses but in the nearby Upper Sulphur Hot Springs, where the water temperature often reaches 40 degrees Celsius. The rest of the Cave and Basin has been restored to appear much as it did a century ago. Visitors can still follow the low entranceway to the dimly lit cave the surveyors discovered, or dip a finger into the slightly warmer waters of the old basin.

There is also much to see outside the buildings. The Discovery Trail follows the trickling streams of warm water up the hill to where they emerge from the mountainside. These hot springs begin as rainwater and melting snow that filter more than 2 kilometres down through the ground on the other side of the mountain. Warmed by heat radiating from the earth's molten interior, the now mineralized and pressurized water flows back to the surface along the Sulphur Mountain fault line.

The emerging hot springs deposit calcium carbonate, dissolved from the limestone bedrock during the water's underground migration. These deposits form soft, porous rock

Looking northeast from the Marsh Trail to Mount Inglismaldie.

known as tufa, which over thousands of years has accumulated to a depth of 7 metres here.

The hot mineral waters, with their distinctive odour, flow down the hillside, feeding the Cave and Basin and the Vermilion wetlands below. This unique habitat can be visited by following the looping 500-metre Marsh Trail on a boardwalk below the Cave and Basin. The constant supply of warm water allows watercress to grow year-round and inspires robins, killdeer and mallard ducks to forego their usual migrations. From spring through fall, a large variety of other water birds can be spotted on the marsh from a wooden blind.

This warm wetland was also the home of the Banff longnose dace, a minnow unique to the area. Unfortunately, the introduction of competing tropical fish in the 1960s may well have precipitated the dace's demise. It was declared extinct in 1991.

Banff Park Museum

Western Canada's oldest natural history museum is well worth visiting for its unusual architecture and impressive wildlife collection. It also serves as a reminder of how park values have changed over the decades.

The Banff Park Museum was built in 1903, replacing a smaller museum erected across the river in 1895. The building represents a so-called railroad pagoda style of architecture, featuring cross-log construction, a lantern skylight and interior panelling of Douglas fir.

The museum was originally intended to attract wealthy tourists and introduce them to wild creatures that were safely stuffed. Students of natural history were also attracted to this "University of the Hills."

The museum's earliest specimen is an 1860 merganser duck. Most of the other wildlife was collected early last century from various parts of the world, including the park. Though the hunting of game animals such as elk and bighorn sheep was banned within the park in 1890, a predator control program continued for some decades, claiming the lives of wolves, coyotes, eagles and owls, some of which ended up in the museum. Other specimens were once residents of a zoo and aviary that operated from 1904 to 1937 on the museum grounds and contained such exotic species as a polar bear and turkey vulture.

Times have changed and the emphasis now is on viewing animals and birds in their natural surroundings. The collection, however, has more recently benefitted from the considerable road kill on the park's highways.

Perhaps the museum's most compelling exhibit is a huge grizzly skin. It comes from a garbage-addicted bear that in 1980 killed one person and mauled three others on the town's doorstep before being snared and shot. The bullet hole is clearly visible between the bear's eyes.

Tunnel Mountain Drive

ROUTE: From its intersection with Banff Avenue (just north of the Bow River Bridge), follow Buffalo Street east as it angles right to become Tunnel Mountain Drive. At 4 kilometres, turn right on Tunnel Mountain Road, which passes the hoodoos en route to its junction with Banff Avenue at Rocky Mountain Resort. **DRIVING DISTANCE:** 10 kilometres one way.

Tunnel Mountain Drive is perhaps the finest short drive in the vicinity of Banff townsite. It climbs along the side of Tunnel Mountain, passing numerous pull-offs that offer superb views up and down the Bow Valley. Along the way is an optional hike to Tunnel's summit and a short walk overlooking the hoodoos.

The construction of Tunnel Mountain Drive began in the late 1880s as a continuation of Buffalo Street. Trees were cleared and rock dynamited to create a roadway for horse-drawn tallyhos up the hillside above the Bow River. One tightly winding section had to be removed following the official introduction of cars to the park in the mid-1910s.

The road initially climbs to a viewpoint overlooking Bow Falls and the Banff Springs Hotel. The falls have cut into the intersection of two geological formations. The rocks along the Bow River's north banks are some 75 million years older than the Sulphur Mountain siltstones on the south. Smooth-plated siltstones from this formation were used in the construction of the Banff Springs Hotel and the nearby park administration building.

From a parking lot at 1.2 kilometres, a 4.8-kilometre trail descends to follow the Bow River to the hoodoos. The river can be reached, where the Spray River enters, more directly on a steep, slippery trail from the same parking lot. Across the swiftly flowing Bow, one can see the golf course fairways, a favoured dining spot for elk. Nearby, on this side of the river, is a magnificent stand of ancient Douglas fir, their massive, furrowed trunks decorated with mosses.

Back on the road, you soon pass the Banff Centre campus. Its roots go back to 1933 when my great-uncle, E.A. Corbett, started a summer theatre school. Under the guidance of his successor, Donald Cameron, it became the world-renowned Banff School of Fine Arts. Today the Banff Centre also boasts a school of management, a summer-long arts festival, an international television festival and a mountain film festival.

At 2.5 kilometres, the road crosses the Tunnel Mountain trail. From this junction, it's a 1.5-kilometre hike up through lodgepole pine and Douglas fir to the summit, once topped by a fire lookout. Though the climb is steady, the view east down the Bow Valley and over the Fairholme Range is ample reward.

Mount Rundle, to the southeast, was once attached to Tunnel Mountain until glaciers cut a notch, subsequently deepened by the Bow River into a valley, between the two. The Bow is thought to have previously detoured around the north side of Tunnel Mountain, following the Cascade River and Minnewanka Lake valleys before rejoining the current channel on the plains. Some 10,000 years ago, receding glaciers deposited moraines that blocked that channel and created a lake to the west. The lake's accumulating meltwaters eventually spilled through the notch between Rundle and Tunnel to form the new channel.

Tunnel Mountain seems a misnomer on two counts. A planned tunnel through the mountain was scrapped in 1883 when the Canadian Pacific Railway line was detoured north. But the name stuck. At a mere 1,690 metres (5,550 feet), Tunnel also scarcely qualifies as a real mountain in the Canadian Rockies, though the tall cliffs on the south and east faces are certainly impressive.

Farther along Tunnel Mountain Drive are pull-offs with less lofty but still inspiring views west along the Bow Valley and north to Cascade Mountain and the ski slopes of Mount

Norquay. At a cluster of condominiums, the road turns right and follows a dry, open terrace dotted with trees. It is a typical montane forest environment, attracting grazing elk and mule deer.

For 2 kilometres, the road passes the Tunnel Mountain Campgrounds, the largest such facility in the mountain national parks, with more than 1,150 sites. When the campground was first moved here from the golf course area in the 1930s, some citizens complained it was too far removed from the town's businesses. Townsfolk are no doubt glad of its distance today, given its size and reputation for late-night revelry.

The road soon reaches the hoodoos. A 500-metre asphalt trail (wheelchair accessible) follows the northeast bank of the Bow River and leads to viewpoints overlooking the hoodoos. Hoodoo is apparently a variation of voodoo, reflecting the often fantastic shapes they assume. Interpretive signs explain how running water has washed away the hard slopes of glacially deposited till, leaving behind these isolated pillars. But their once protective caps have disappeared, exposing them, too, to the relentless forces of erosion.

Lake Minnewanka Loop

ROUTE: From the Trans-Canada Highway interchange at the east entrance to Banff townsite, drive north past Bankhead to Lake Minnewanka. From the lake, continue the loop to Two Jack Lake and back to the highway.
DRIVING DISTANCE: 16 kilometres return.

Lake Minnewanka, the largest lake in Banff National Park, is one of the most popular destinations in the area. Its charms can be discovered in an hour or so, a trip extended by visiting an abandoned coal mining community, walking up a narrow canyon, or having a picnic. The lake can also be toured by boat and its depths plumbed by hook for lake trout.

From the Trans-Canada Highway, the road passes beneath the impressive folds of Cascade Mountain, named for the waterfall that splits its face. The coal seams at the mountain's base were first mined at the beginning of the century to help power the Canadian Pacific Railway's engines. The resulting mining town of Bankhead prospered, supporting a population of 1,000 at its peak. But by 1922, the mine had closed, the victim of difficult mining conditions, poor markets and labour unrest.

Many of Bankhead's buildings were demolished or moved to Banff or Canmore. But the mining site can still be toured on a short interpretive trail leading down from the Lower Bankhead parking lot. Just up the road, the Upper Bankhead parking lot provides access to further remains of concrete foundations.

Beyond Bankhead, the road soon leads to Lake Minnewanka. The Minnewanka Valley likely once cradled a stretch of the Bow River as it surged out of the mountains. The channel was abandoned some 10,000 years ago, when an overflowing glacial lake to the west carved a new course between Mount Rundle and Tunnel Mountain.

The valley has also long been a major transportation corridor. The Stoney first used it as an entry to the mountains, a route followed in the mid-1800s by explorers, missionaries and even settlers bound for Oregon. In the late 1880s, a road was built from Banff to Lake Minnewanka, ushering in an era of tourism that remains unabated.

Early on, the small resort community of Minnewanka Landing was built along the near shore and tour boat operations were launched. A hydroelectric dam built at the lake's outlet in 1912 and expanded in 1941, however, raised the water levels by nearly 25 metres and extended the lake's length by 8 kilometres. The resort was abandoned, its foundations today visited only by fish and scuba divers.

But tourism is resilient. Visitors still flock here to walk the shores or take a boat cruise to Devil's Gap at the east end of the lake. Anglers in small boats troll for sizable lake trout, though the catches are considerably less than at the turn of the century.

North of the parking lot is a concession and picnic area frequented by bighorn sheep. Just beyond, a trail along Lake Minnewanka's northwest shore leads through pine and fir forest to soon cross Stewart Canyon on a large wooden-truss bridge. A short side trail leads up this impressive limestone gorge, where the Cascade River enters the lake.

In 1841, George Simpson, governor of the Hudson's Bay Company, called it Peechee Lake after his native guide who lived along the shore. A more enduring name was Devil's Lake, used by both native inhabitants and early white visitors. In 1916, it was renamed Minnewanka, meaning "lake of the water spirit."

From the Lake Minnewanka parking lot, the road continues across an earth-filled dam to a viewpoint overlooking the lake before dropping past Two Jack Lake. At a junction, a spur road leads left to Johnson Lake, crossing en route a canal carrying water from Lake Minnewanka down to the Cascade power plant on the Trans-Canada Highway. Johnson Lake, ringed by a trail, is a tranquil spot for a picnic and birdwatching. Return to the junction and turn left to regain the Lake Minnewanka Road, which leads back to Banff.

Lake Louise

ROUTE: From the Canada Olympic Park traffic lights, drive 170 kilometres west on the Trans-Canada Highway to the Lake Louise exit. Lake Louise is reached by a 4-kilometre paved road, which also provides access, via a 12-kilometre spur road, to Moraine Lake. From Banff, an alternative and much quieter route to Lake Louise is the Bow Valley Parkway.

Lake Louise probably boasts more tourists per scenic square metre than any place in the Canadian Rockies. Yet the alpine splendour of this mountain setting remains largely undiminished. It is even possible, with a little effort, to escape the hordes that troop to this alpine mecca.

This trip visits the two "must-do" highlights, Lake Louise and Moraine Lake, and offers a couple of short walks to complete a most pleasant day. If you want to see the sights in relative quiet, it's best to either get underway very early or arrive in the late afternoon.

The Stoney called Lake Louise the "Lake of Little Fishes." It was briefly named Emerald Lake by its first white visitor, Canadian Pacific Railway surveyor Tom Wilson, led here by Stoney guide Edwin Hunter in 1882.

Keen to attract rail-travelling tourists to the mountains, the Canadian Pacific Railway erected the Lake Louise Chalet at this exquisite location in 1890. When this small structure burned down three years later, it was quickly replaced by a second chalet. Several wings were added over the next 20 years to accommodate a steady increase in summer visitors, who were now arriving by road in horse-drawn carriages and, later, by a tramline ascending from the Laggan train station. A second fire destroyed much of the building in 1924, but a new wing was built within a year. Subsequent additions and renovations have made Chateau Lake Louise into a major mountain hotel and convention centre.

Beyond the lake's far shore shines Mount Victoria. Its long snowy ridge is a classic alpine climb, usually tackled from a high stone hut named after Philip Abbott, the first climber killed in the Rockies. His death on nearby Mount Lefroy in 1896 prompted the CPR to import Swiss guides to safely lead wealthy foreign climbers, men and women, up the area's peaks.

To escape the throngs that congregate along the lake's shores, take the 1-kilometre hike from behind the boathouse

Chateau Lake Louise from Fairview Lookout.

to Fairview Lookout. Soon you will be enveloped in the silence of a mossy forest of spruce and fir. The steepness of the slope and its northern aspect shield the forest from sun and wind and thus allow it to retain moisture. As you ascend this Cadillac trail, consider the plight of early explorers bushwacking over the deadfall and hummocky ground.

A signed trail to the right rises to a small lookout high above Lake Louise and the chateau. Far below, tiny tourists trek along the lakeshore, many bound for an alpine tea house. The lake's colour turns in spring from a bluish hue to milky green. The milky colour is the result of rock flour—rocks ground by glaciers into a fine dust—deposited by meltwater in the lake, where it reflects every colour but the emerald you see. The small glacier at the head of nearby Moraine Lake is not actively feeding the lake, so retains a more consistent blue throughout the year.

If time permits, it's well worth visiting Moraine Lake, a short drive away. The lake's blue waters reflect a wall of glaciated peaks that constitute one end of the Valley of Ten Peaks. In 1894, American climber Samuel Allen named these peaks after Stoney numerals 1 to 10. Today, only the ninth and tenth peaks, Neptuak and Wenkchemna, retain those Stoney names. If you look closely at the cliffs across the lake, you can make out the horizontal layers of limestone on top of shale on top of sandstone.

The near end of the lake is dammed by a jumble of boulders, deposited either by a rock slide or an ancient glacier. A short interpretive trail leads to the top of this rock pile, from which the picture that graces Canada's old 20-dollar bill was taken. Along the way, you can learn about ripple marks and trilobite tracks in rocks that trace their origins to sands and muds transported from as far away as Manitoba and deposited in a 500-million-year-old inland sea.

Moraine Lake is thronged with tourists throughout the summer. In late September, many hikers make the 3-kilometre pilgrimage up to Larch Valley to see the deciduous alpine larch needles that have turned to orange.

Unfortunately, not all trees are treated as reverentially here. On one visit to Moraine Lake, I saw workers felling spruce with a chainsaw, undoubtedly to improve the views from a lakeside lodge that, like many developments in the national park, has seen recent expansions.

Burgess Shale Hike

ROUTE: From the Canada Olympic Park traffic lights, drive 193 kilometres west on the Trans-Canada Highway to the Yoho Valley Road, and follow it 15 kilometres north to the Takakkaw Falls parking lot.
DRIVING DISTANCE: 208 kilometres one way.

NOTE: The Burgess Shale and Mount Stephen fossil beds are closed to visitors except those on a Yoho-Burgess Shale Foundation guided hike, offered from early July to late September. The 10-hour Burgess Shale guided hike is 21 kilometres return and gains 750 metres in elevation ($45 for adults and $25 for children under 12). The 6.5-hour Mount Stephen hike is 6 kilometres return and rises 520 metres in elevation ($25 for adults and $15 for children under 12). Participants should be reasonably fit. Phone 1-800-343-3006 for reservations and information or check http://www.burgess-shale.bc.ca/.

The Burgess Shale, a UNESCO World Heritage Site, is arguably the most important fossil discovery in the world. It exquisitely preserves an abundance and diversity of 500-million-year-old marine organisms and provides a unique insight into how animal life appeared on earth.

The only way to legally see these fossils up close is on a guided hike, either a full day trip to the Burgess Shale high on Mount Field (the trip described here) or a shorter excursion to the nearby trilobite beds on Mount Stephen, above the town of Field, B.C. It's a terrific opportunity to learn in detail about this fossil record from a paleontologist or geologist, perhaps spot researchers at work and enjoy the alpine splendour of Yoho National Park along the way.

Burgess Shale hikers convene across from Takakkaw Falls ("magnificent" in Cree), Canada's third-highest waterfall, which funnels meltwaters from the Daly Glacier into a thunderous free fall of 254 metres. From its start near the youth hostel, the century-old trail climbs steeply through heavy timber and then levels out shortly before reaching tiny Yoho Lake, overshadowed by the impressive north face of Wapta Mountain. Just beyond, the trail swings south at the forested Yoho Pass and traverses beneath Wapta's steep limestone cliffs, offering stellar views over the Emerald Valley to Michael Peak, Mount Carnarvon and Noseeum Falls. An airy trailside luncheon spot looks nearly 900 metres down to vibrant Emerald Lake and its upscale lodge. Not far from Burgess Pass, only guided hikers are allowed to turn east off the main trail for a final steep climb to the Walcott Quarry, just below the north ridge of Mount Field (video cameras are apparently used to detect unauthorized visitors).

The quarry is named for Charles Walcott, head of the Smithsonian Institution when he stumbled on these rich fossil beds in 1909. (The Mount Stephen beds, across the highway, were investigated by R.G. McConnell of the Geological Survey of Canada in 1886 after railway workers discovered an abundance of trilobite fossils.) Walcott and family members spent the next decade excavating the quarry and hauling some 65,000 fossils away to Washington, D.C. The good news is that this and surrounding quarries have produced about

Guided hikers inspect the Burgess Shale's Walcott Quarry.

200,000 fossils to date, with many more to be uncovered by ongoing scientific research. The continued excavation of fossils in a national park, researchers argue, is justified by its considerable contribution to scientific knowledge.

This abundance of fossils in such a confined area is a miracle of evolutionary and geological forces. The Burgess Shale animals lived more than 500 million years ago on a large carbonate reef, called the Cathedral Escarpment, at the edge of the ancient North American continent in a warm, shallow sea. Occasional mudslides would sweep over the escarpment, burying and instantly killing organisms and allowing their preservation to begin immediately. Over the next 250 million years, these fossils became buried under about 10 kilometres of accumulated sediments, which hardened into rocks that were eventually thrust up into today's mountains. Despite incredible pressures, heat and erosion over this time, these fossils somehow survived, encased in shale.

Most animal fossils found elsewhere retain hard bits such as shells and skeletons. The Burgess Shale is unique in its beautiful preservation of soft body parts such as feathery gills, muscle bands and even guts. It also harbours more than 120 fossilized marine animal species, a number of which had never been seen before. These species range from the numerous and striking trilobites and marellas, or lace crabs, to the five-eyed opabinia, the flower-like dinomischus and the worm-like pikaia, which with its primitive spinal chord is our oldest known ancestor.

Because of this well-preserved diversity of fossils, the Burgess Shale has helped shape scientific understanding of how life has evolved. In particular, it provides the most complete fossilized record of the so-called Cambrian explosion more than 500 million years ago, when many complex animal forms—including those with segmented bodies, jointed limbs and spinal chords—appeared over a relatively short 10-20 million years. The Burgess Shale thus provides a snapshot of an evolutionary outburst that dominated the world's oceans over the next 300 million years.

Although truckloads of Burgess Shale and Mount Stephen fossils have been shipped to far-flung museums over the years, there are plans to repatriate some of those fossils and keep new discoveries in a facility in Field. Monies from the guided hikes and other fund-raising initiatives are being collected to build a learning centre/museum to accommodate various educational groups as well as researchers.

While in the small mountain community of Field (population 300), it's worth stopping at one of several good restaurants or staying at a bed and breakfast or inn. Established in 1885 during construction of the Canadian Pacific Railway, Field remains a division point for the railway and is the headquarters for Yoho National Park.

Index